Sweeten the Pot

How to Leverage Incentives and Rebates to Drive Loyalty and Increase Profits

Ben Wieder

Limit of Liability/Disclaimer of Warranties

ISBN: 978-1-7332277-0-4

I'd like to dedicate this book to my three favorite ladies, Rachel, Anna, and Sarah. You've been my bedrock of daily support for years, and I truly appreciate you for believing in me.

Contents

Foreword 1

Chapter 1: What is an Incentive? 5

Incentives and Economics 7

Rational Choice Theory 9

Moving to a Behavioral Economics Model 10

Behavioral Economics and Business 11

It's the Incentives, Stupid 13

What Is an Incentive? 14

Positive vs. Negative Incentives 17

Carrots and Sticks 20

Making Incentives Work for You 23

Increasing Engagement 24

Case Studies: Incentives as Game Changers 26

Reward Options for Employee Incentives 28

Chapter 2: Behavior Modification 31

Incentives as Behavior Modification 32

Quotas and Caps: Enemies of Progress 34

The Case of the Cabbies 37

What's the Right Reward? 38

Don't Let Your Ego Get in the Way 42

Staying Up to Date 44

Chapter 3: Employee Incentive Rewards

    Vs. Recognition Awards   49

Incentive Rewards 51

Reloadable Branded Debit Cards 56

Recognition Awards 58

Combining Incentive Rewards and Recognition Awards 61

Chapter 4: Calculating ROI for Incentive Programs...................... 65

Traditional Advertising...66

Direct Mail..68

Digital Marketing...69

Sales and Discounts 78

Incentive Program ROI..80

Chapter 5: The Training Option 87

Drinking the Kool-Aid 88

Employee Education 90

Chapter 6: Salesperson Incentives 97

Sales Incentives for Channel Marketing..........................99

Using Salesperson Incentives for the Right Products.......... 105

Remember Your Target Market........................... 107

Chapter 7: Incentives for Employee Behavior 109

Incentivizing Employee Behavior......................... 112

Chapter 8: Incentives for Customers: Rebate Programs 123

Customer Rebates as Incentives........................ 124

Increasing Brand Affinity 128

Chapter 9: Customer Loyalty Programs 131

Stay On Their Minds 132

The Technical Side of Customer Loyalty Programs.............. 133

What a Customer Loyalty Program Can Do........................ 135

Tips for an Effective Customer Loyalty Program.................. 137

Chapter 10: Incentive Type: Branded Reloadable,
           Prepaid, and Virtual Debit Cards   143

Reloadable Branded Debit Card 146

Prepaid Branded Debit Card (aka Rebate Card)................. 149

Virtual Debit Cards 150

Chapter 11: Merchandise and Travel... 155

Cash or Merchandise & Travel? 156

How to Implement Merchandise and Travel Programs 160

Inspiring Photos and Testimonials 165

Brand Affinity 166

Chapter 12: What to Look for (and Avoid) in a Bank 169

Banks and Incentives 170

What to Look for in a Bank 171

What to Avoid in a Bank: A Cautionary Tale 172

Chapter 13: How to Design an Incentive program 177

Identifying the Players 178

Identifying Your Goals 179

Setting Expectations 180

Creating a Timeline 182

Getting Approved by a Bank 184

Chapter 14: Do I Need a Web Portal? 189

Benefits of Having a Web Portal 190

Integration with Existing User Portals 192

Single-sign-on Web Portals 193

Do I Need a Mobile App? 194

When Do I Not Need a Web Portal? 196

Chapter 15: Working with a Management Partner 199

Should I Hire an Outside Firm? 200

What to Look for in a Management Partner 204

Chapter 16: How Much Do Incentive Programs Cost? 209

How Incentive Firms Handle Pricing 212

Payment Terms for Incentive Companies 215

Chapter 17: Taxes and Incentive Programs 219

Incentives, Rewards, Cash, and Taxes 221

Incentive Rewards and Employee Tax Liability 222

Incentives and Non-Employees 224

Are Points Worth Something? 227

Rebates and Taxes..230

Incentive Rewards and Our Own Taxes 230

Chapter 18: Paying Out Third-party Rewards 233

Paying Incentives to Business Owners or Dealer Principals. 234

Issuing Rewards Directly to Salespeople 236

Recipient Conflict...237

Chapter 19: Program Launch & Rollout.................................239

Launching a Program with Independent Dealers................240

Chapter 20: Incentive Program Best Practices 243

Be Consistent, But Keep Things Fresh 245

Take the Stairs..246

Spin & Win 247

Keep It Simple 248

Communication Is Key 249

Make It Worth Their While 250

Remember the Incentives vs. Recognition Distinction 251

Focus on Your Goals...253

Do Your Homework..255

Don't Overlook Security 256

Be Careful When Choosing a Bank................................257

Work With a Management Partner................................258

Endnotes 261

Foreword

When I first told my friends and family that I was writing a business book, the common response was something along the lines of: "Oh, so you're writing a marketing book?" True, I memorized television commercials as a child, studied marketing in college, and own Level 6, a respected marketing firm, but I figure there's enough standard-issue marketing books to circle the earth a few times over. Plus, there just happens to be one specific aspect of marketing that I know more about than 99.9% of my peers: Incentive programs.

I didn't enter the world of incentives with specific intent. In fact, as I often say, Level 6 fell into this space "back asswards." Back in the mid-2000s, a large client asked if we could design and implement a full, turnkey sales incentive program for them. They'd never done one previously, and neither had we. And they had exactly 8 weeks to develop the entire thing. None of this stopped us from trying. My first stop? The local bookstore. I figured there had to be several books written on this subject, and the knowledge within would give us a jump start on designing a great program. Unfortunately, there was nothing available.

Somehow, through sheer grit and determination, we figured out how to build amazing, custom incentive programs. After several years and many clients, we've issued millions of dollars of incentives for our clients, leading to significant ROI in multiple industries. Did we make some mistakes along the way? Probably. But we've saved our clients money and made their lives easier, all while perfecting our services to where they are today.

About a year ago, I searched Amazon again, thinking there must be a great resource book for incentive programs, especially with their rising popularity. But again, there was nothing, thus spawning the idea for *Sweeten the Pot*.

As I often say, developing incentive programs isn't rocket science. You don't need a PhD. from MIT or an MBA from Harvard. However, there are many mysteries and unknowns for those who don't dabble in this space every day. If you're reading this book, chances are good that your job duties, the ones that you're actually evaluated upon, involve tasks quite different than fulfilling rebate cards, programming incentive websites, or issuing 1099 tax forms. If that's the case, great. Our team has developed this book specifically to those who need to lead the development of these programs.

Even when you finish this book and launch your new program, your primary responsibilities likely still won't be fulfilling rebate cards, programming incentive websites, or issuing 1099 tax forms. That said, you'll know how to build the right type of program, with the right offers, the right technology, and most importantly, the right team.

And now a word of warning. While I've written this book to be a reference guide, the first few chapters are largely philosophical in nature. They deal with topics such as economic theory, behavioral modification, and understanding the conceptual difference between incentive rewards and recognition awards. While not necessary to those who only want the nuts and bolts, I feel this information is invaluable to those who desire a deeper understanding of the "why" behind incentive programs. While this early content is largely scholastic in nature, I strongly feel it's worth getting through. With this foundational knowledge, you'll be better prepared to identify the appropriate program for your unique audience.

I'd like to personally thank my entire team for their continued support. Special thanks to Darcy St. George, Katie Rudolph, Arelda Shkurti, Matt Coffay, Doug Williams, Kim Jory, Katrina Kane, Chris Protzmann, and Claudine Raschi. I couldn't have done this book without your guidance.

Finally, I'd like to thank you, the reader, for taking time out of your busy schedule to read this book. I sincerely hope that it feeds you with the knowledge you'll need to design and develop a successful incentive program for your organization.

Chapter 1

What Is an Incentive?

Inventor and entrepreneur Elon Musk was born uncere-moniously in South Africa in 1971. A precocious child, at the age of only 17 he decided to move to Canada and study at Queen's University. A few years later, he transferred to the University of Pennsylvania with an ambitious dual-study path of economics and physics. Soon after, he pursued a Ph.D. at Stanford in applied physics, but famously quit that program after only two days to start his first software company, Zip2. After he sold that company, he founded an online bank that would eventually become PayPal. PayPal would be acquired for $1.5 billion, and he then decided to build spaceships at his new company SpaceX. His many other ventures include his widely known electric car company Tesla.

OK, so you probably already knew a lot of this, and you certainly didn't pick up this book to learn about Elon Musk. But why did he decide to move to leave South Africa in the first place? How did he decide to quit Stanford shortly after starting? And why in the world did he decide to develop spaceships, tunnels and self-driving cars? The answer is this: We don't really know. And Elon Musk probably doesn't know with 100% certainty either.

Why do any of us do the things we do?

Why do researchers at universities invent new technologies[1] that can dramatically change the way we interact with the world? Why do employees at specific companies[2] go above and beyond at work, increasing revenue and market share for a business they don't own? Why do you buy a specific brand of toothpaste when you're at the grocery store? How did you decide on the clothes you're wearing today?

To make the point plainly: Why are you reading this book right now?

Let's face it, humans are complicated creatures. The left hemisphere of our brain[3] quietly, or sometimes forcefully, reminds us to make decisions rationally. It tells us that we ought to think things through, weigh the pros and cons, take existing evidence into account, and ultimately come to a conclusion based on facts and evidence.

Meanwhile, the right hemisphere pushes back—and pushes back hard. While we're busy trying to account for all the logical reasons that a given decision is the "correct" one for us, the right hemisphere—the part of the brain responsible for emotions, creativity, and big-picture thinking—pulls us in the opposite direction. Why? Because that direction is often more fun and feels better.

In fact, just about any attempt to analyze human behavior is going to involve an investigation of how these opposing internal forces—the rational and the emotional, to put it simply—end up playing themselves out. How do we negotiate the competition between what information instructs us to do and what desire draws us toward?

What if information and desire weren't in competition? When a particular course of action is both logical (making sense on paper with a measurable outcome that's subjectively positive) *and* emotionally satisfying (feeling good to be doing it), it's safe to assume that the average person is going to follow that course of action in 99.9% of cases.

When you give people something that makes both their logical, rational, parochial left brain and their emotional, feeling, creative right brain happy, you can directly influence their choices, performance, and attitude. When you're helping people feel good about their decisions on multiple levels, their behavior becomes a lot easier to predict. As you'll see throughout this book, that's exactly what incentives do for us.

Incentives and Economics

Before we go any further, let's back up a little. We've acknowledged that humans are complicated creatures. But are there any important sectors of human life where logic wins out 100% of the time and humans really do fill the shoes of their Aristotelian label as the "rational animal?"

According to most classical and neoclassical economists, there's no real tension in the human mind when it comes to people as economic actors. If you're not familiar with economics, you might be surprised to hear this. Isn't this totally at odds with our actual life experiences? If people are completely rational creatures when it comes to all their decisions surrounding consumption—like which smartphone to buy or which brand of car to drive—what's up with the advertising industry? Aren't those guys going about it all wrong, hitting people with one emotional appeal after another in an attempt to sell as many widgets as they can?

Common sense tells us that people don't make all their economic decisions the same way that they solve math problems. We know from experience that humans are much more complicated and emotional than that.

Believe it or not, though, economists have argued precisely the opposite for years. Up until recently, the average economist would have tried to convince you that humans were little more than rational actors, looking to maximize their economic utility; that is, consume and spend in the most rational way possible. While there are still plenty of so-called experts in the field who will toe this line, this false conception of human economic behavior has lost traction over the last couple of decades, thanks to something called behavioral economics.

Let's take a closer look at what the average economist used to believe about how human beings make decisions.

Rational Choice Theory

Previously, virtually every economist subscribed to an idea known as rational choice theory.[4] According to this economic theory, people only make decisions pertaining to their economic lives in a rational, logical way.

How does this play out? In theory, we take all extenuating factors and information into account before making decisions, like those for jobs or product purchases.

Should I work some extra hours this week? Maybe. Let me think it through and come to a purely rational, numbers-based decision. Things such as how I'm feeling, how much I dislike my boss, or how much money I want to spend during the weekend won't be taken into account.

Which make and model of car do I want to buy? According to rational choice theory, I'm going to go with the one that's the most logical choice based on my current circumstances. In other words, there's no way I'd ever go for the impractical sports car when I've got a family to think about. And there's certainly no way I'd purchase a V-8 powered SUV when a 4-cylinder economy car would get me from point A to point B with better fuel economy.

As you probably know, this isn't how people make decisions. People don't do the things that they do for purely rational, logical reasons. Other assumptions have to come into play here. For example, we must assume that people have access to perfect and complete information in order to make these perfectly complete and rational decisions.

It's pretty easy to see how absurd this purely logical thought process can be.

Moving to a Behavioral Economics Model

Beginning in the 1950s, people started to challenge the purely rational way of thinking.

One of the first was noted economist Herbert Simon. According to his bounded rationality model,[5] Simon argued that people simply don't have access to the perfect information that would cause them to always make rational decisions in their best interests. This may seem obvious to us today, but it was a rather groundbreaking suggestion at the time.

In the decades that followed, psychologists started weighing in. In particular, Gerd Gigerenzer, Daniel Kahneman, and Avos Tversky[6] won the Nobel prize in economics for their work on heuristics in human decision making. Essentially, they claimed that humans don't really think through every decision from beginning to end. Instead, they use shortcuts—heuristics—to make decisions.

This really is straightforward when you think about it. Without heuristics, it'd be pretty difficult to make any decisions about how to go about your day. You'd spend so much time trying to decide what to have for lunch that you'd never make it to your afternoon meeting. In fact, you may end up going hungry due to such slow decision making.

Thinking Fast and Slow

Coming up to the turn of the century and beyond, economics has seen a massive shift. The neoclassical model of the rational, fully informed, 100% logical human subject is no longer in style. In fact, taking this model for granted could get you laughed at in some economics circles, although by no means in all of them. (Some economists continue to hold onto these false assumptions.)

Kahneman and Tversky are considered to be among some of the founding thinkers of what's now generally referred to as behavioral economics. Kahneman claims that we actually do our decision making in two separate states of mind: Type 1, or "fast," thinking, and Type 2, or "slow," thinking.[7] As it turns out, most of our activity is habitual, Type 1 thinking. We don't take the time to reason our way through every situation that's presented to us. And, even when we make the switch over to Type 2 thinking and opt to really puzzle our way through a situation, we ultimately may find ourselves switching back to Type 1 thinking. Why? Because there's too much information, and too little time. In the end, and as we'll discuss further, most of our decision making is a combination of emotion and habit.

So, what does this mean for you as a businessperson? As we'll see, it means a lot.

Behavioral Economics and Business

It's hard to point to a single book, paper, or lecture that really turned the economic tide. There are, however, a few significant works that stand out. In addition to Kahneman's *Thinking Fast and Slow*, Thaler and Sunstein's *Nudge*[8] points to the way that human behavior—particularly what we'd consider to be so-called economic behavior—can be manipulated with the proper nudge in the right direction.

According to Sunstein and Thaler, there's no such thing as a "neutral" setting for someone to make a decision. That's just another economic abstraction (read: falsehood) from the days of old. Instead, we all find ourselves in some sort of context whenever it comes time to make a decision. Whether you're an employee deciding whether to put in a little extra work to reach a goal, or a cash-strapped 20-something shopping at the grocery store, your context is going to play an important role in your decision making.

Here's the thing about those contexts, though: Sunstein and Thaler found that small changes in an environment or experience—what we'd otherwise probably consider to be too insignificant to have any real impact on an individual's decision making—could completely alter people's habits and choices.

Sunstein and Thaler call this "libertarian paternalism." If that looks a little bit like a contradiction, you're right: It is. But Sunstein and Thaler intended it that way. What they meant to communicate is a concept that combines leaving free will intact and letting people make their own decisions with giving them a nudge in the right direction to help them make the best one possible.

In *Nudge*, they give all sorts of examples of how this approach can be put to use for people's benefit. Don't make people opt-in to their 401(k) plan: enroll them automatically and make them opt out. Automatically rebalance portfolios, rather than forcing clients to request it. These sorts of approaches are important for one simple reason: people are often lazy, so it's often easier to do nothing than to do something.

Following that same line of thinking, then, modifying human behavior seems like a Herculean task. If people are inherently lazy (Sunstein and Thaler prefer the term "inertia" to "laziness," but let's be honest here), and if decision making is largely contextual, then how do we change people's behaviors?

How do I get my sales team to break this quarter's goal?

How can I convince a distributor to promote my product more than my competitor's?

What can I do to create shopping habits with customers, so that they don't wander away back into the wilderness of the free market?

The answer? Incentives. Powerful, compelling, logical-emotional, habit-creating incentives.

It's the Incentives, Stupid

In 2005, Steven Levitt and Stephen Dubner released a book called *Freakonomics*. It's hard to overstate how important this book was in changing the way that many modern economists think—and it was a popular bestseller to boot.

As Levitt and Dubner point out in the introduction to their sequel,[9] *Superfreakonomics*, the book really comes down to one thing. "If pressed, you could boil [the main idea of the book] down to four words: People respond to incentives."

Throughout the book, Levitt and Dubner essentially argue that economics is all about incentives. We may not realize it, but the vast majority of our behavior is incentives-driven.

According to the authors, incentives are the "cornerstone of modern life." If you want to solve "just about any riddle"—whatever that riddle may be—understanding how incentives work is essential to making it happen. If you don't understand what incentives are, how they work, and why they matter, then you're going to have a tough time grappling with modern economic realities.

What is an Incentive?

Simply put, an incentive is any external factor that influences our behavior in a predictable way.

We're exposed to incentives from a very young age, and they take a variety of forms. Levitt and Dubner characterize incentives by type, arguing that incentives can be economic, moral, or social. They're not mutually exclusive, though. It's possible for someone to be influenced by social, moral, and economic incentives at the same time. For example, consider some of the reasons why the average person might abstain from committing a crime:

- Moral incentive: we've been taught that committing a crime is morally wrong.

- Social incentive: if we commit a crime, we may experience judgment and social exclusion from others.

- Economic incentive: if we're caught, we might be fined, jailed, or lose our job.

On the surface, incentives seem fairly straightforward. You give someone a reason to do something, and they do it. That's not complicated, is it?

It's true: on the one hand, incentives are deceptively simple. At the same time, though, it's possible to understand what incentives are, but still struggle when it comes to applying them in real life. This sort of thing happens all the time. Business owners want to put incentives into practice to influence employee and/or customer behavior (something we strongly support if you want to be successful). But things don't always turn out as you'd planned. As Levitt and Dubner readily point out in their book, incentives may not have the desired effect if they're executed incorrectly.

Let's look at an example from *Freakonomics*. Levitt and Dubner cite the case of a daycare center that was having issues with parents showing up late to pick up their children. At the end of the day, daycare workers were being forced to sit around for hours on end, waiting for a handful of parents to show up. The daycare wanted to come up with a way to fix this problem, and they decided to create what we'd call a negative incentive to discourage the behavior (more on negative vs. positive incentives later).

What was the negative incentive? Simply put, any parent who failed to show up on time would be forced to pay a

$3 fine. For parents with children in daycare five days a week, that could quickly add up to an extra $50 or more each month. The daycare assumed that, after being fined a couple of times, parents would get their acts together and pick up their kids on time.

So, what was the outcome? The results might surprise you. Not only did the fine fail to discourage parents from picking up their children when they were supposed to—it actually *made the problem worse*. That's right: within a few weeks, the problem was no longer just a handful of parents showing up late. Before they knew it, large numbers of parents were showing up later than ever to pick up their children.

What was going on here? A couple of things. For one, that $3 fine was too small. If a parent is already paying hundreds (or even thousands) of dollars a month for daycare, an individual fine of $3 is a drop in the bucket. Sure, it *could* add up over the course of a month. Logically speaking, most parents should (in theory) assess the fact that $3 x 20 days is $60 and opt to save $60 by picking up their kids on time. But what have we learned so far? People aren't purely rational creatures when it comes to economic decision making.

On top of the fact that the fine was too small, it turned out that it was actually encouraging parents to leave *their* children late. Why? Well, previously, parents felt that it was their duty to come pick up their children on time. Sure, some parents were routinely late—but the vast majority of them knew that they needed to be there at the agreed-upon hour. There was a social incentive in place there:

they didn't want to do something rude by showing up late. There's also a moral incentive to consider: we know that it's wrong to be irresponsible and fail to stick to an agreement.

With a $3 fine, though, they could suffer a very minor negative economic incentive in exchange for absolving them of the more uncomfortable social and moral incentives. In other words, they suddenly felt fine about leaving their kids at preschool a little later. After all, they are paying a little extra for it, aren't they?

Incentives are powerful, then, and they can have dramatic effects on people's behavior. But not always the effects that we intend. That's why it's important to put the right kinds of incentives in place—at the right time, within the right context, and using the right methods—in order to get the results that you want.

Positive vs. Negative Incentives

What can we learn from the above example when it comes to incentives? It was just an isolated case, after all. So what does it prove?

Uri Gneezy, professor of economics at the University of California, San Diego—and thought leader in the field of behavioral economics—wondered the same. Could this sequence of events be replicated? Was there a causal link between fining parents for being late and the parents showing up even later? Or, was the negative effect of the fine just an unfortunate correlation in this particular case?

Gneezy decided to run an experiment[10] to find out. First, he selected 10 daycares at random in Haifa, Israel. From amongst these 10, he chose 6 to use for his experiment (again, at random), leaving the remaining 4 as a control group. In each of these 6 randomly selected daycares, a fine was introduced for parents who picked their kids up more than 10 minutes later than the agreed upon time on any given day.

Guess what happened? The same thing. Almost immediately, parents began showing up later. In fact, after a given period of time, the number of parents coming to pick their kids up late actually doubled on average. Gneezy managed to reproduce the effect of imposing the fine with almost startling predictability.

So, what's happening here? As we pointed out above, the fine in this instance actually gave parents a sort of economic permission to leave their kids at daycare a little later. While there was a new economic incentive in place for the parents to pick up their kids on time, two other important incentives—a moral one (failing to stick to an agreement is wrong) and a social one (I'll feel embarrassed if I show up late repeatedly)—were actually removed from the equation.

This, in short, is the difference between what we call positive and negative incentives.

As the saying goes, there are two ways to lead a horse. You can dangle a carrot in front of it and encourage it forward—or you can follow behind with a stick, prodding it along repeatedly. Over time, a horse following a carrot will become increasingly fixated on the reward at hand—especially if you allow it to nibble a little here and there. At the same time, a horse being prodded along mile after mile will begin to grow irritated. And, eventually, it's going to kick. Hard.

The metaphor is a good one. Human behavior is surprisingly similar: We typically respond well to rewards, and we react to forceful prodding (physical, mental, emotional, financial) with irritation. Sometimes, we'll actually resist the prodding just for the sake of foiling the plans of whoever's holding the stick. Horses will do the same thing. At some point, they decide they're done being prodded. No more forward movement, period.

In a nutshell, this is how we can characterize the difference between positive and negative incentives. A positive incentive is a dangling carrot. A negative incentive is the unpleasant stick beating our behind.

In the daycare example above, how were the given incentives functioning? Were they positive, or were they negative? Let's take a moment to consider.

Initially, there was no economic incentive involved. If a parent picked up their child late from daycare, no fees were going to be assessed. Suddenly, a negative economic incentive was introduced: if a parent showed up late, they'd have to pay a very small fine. That fine was a stick: the parent knows it's there, standing by, ready to prod them should they show up late.

On the flip side, though, there were actually two positive incentives at play. Prior to the introduction of the negative economic incentive, parents picking up their children late felt guilty. They knew it was morally wrong and socially uncomfortable to arrive after the agreed upon time. Once they could just pay a fine, though, they no longer felt bad about coming 20 minutes (or 2 hours) later than they were supposed to.

Think about this for a moment. The daycare had intended to introduce a negative incentive, but what happened? Instead of being a stick, the fine turned into a carrot. Pay a few dollars, and the parents got 3 things:

1. Absolution from the moral wrong of breaking an agreement,
2. Relief from the social discomfort of showing up late, and
3. Extra time to run errands, grab a cup of coffee, or wrap up their work day—without feeling stressed or in a hurry to be on time.

This example not only demonstrates that sticks don't work all that well; it also shows just how unpredictable incentives can be when framed negatively.

Carrots and Sticks

Ian Ayres, a professor of economics at Yale,[11] decided to explore the idea of reward vs. (potential) punishment in greater detail. In his book *Carrots and Sticks*, Ayres discovered something particularly interesting about incentives. While positive incentives (such as rewards) are a powerful thing, they're usually only effective if implemented in a certain way.

Ayres cites a study from 1981 performed by Richard Thaler[12] at the University of Chicago. In the study, Thaler offered people a choice of two rewards: They could have an apple one year from now, or two apples in 366 days. The vast majority of people chose the two-apple option. Why? Well, if they have to wait a year for their apple, why not wait an extra day and get two? After waiting an entire year, an extra 24 hours doesn't make much of a difference.

Thaler followed up with a second question, though: If you could have an apple now, or two apples sometime tomorrow, which would you prefer? In this case, the vast majority of people reversed their decision. They didn't want to wait until tomorrow. They wanted that apple now. Quick. On the double!

Why? Because humans feel more certainty when a decision is shorter-term in nature.

Just think of all the crazy stuff that could happen between today and tomorrow. You're hungry now, but what if you're stuffed tomorrow when he hands you those two apples? Or, what if you decide you don't like apples? What if you've got a lunch date immediately afterwards, in which case the apples will just sit in your car and spoil from the heat? What if—you get the idea.

A lot of us are prone to worry. Being concerned for the future is an evolved human tendency. In healthy doses, it's a good thing. If we never experienced any anxiety at all, we wouldn't be long for this world. We'd engage in all sorts of risky behavior, and we'd put ourselves into dangerous situations on an hourly basis.

For the majority of people, though, anxiety about the future can get a little out of control. The human aversion to uncertainty is well-documented, something that Ayres' research showed.

So, what does this mean when it comes to incentivizing human behavior?

Simply put, positive incentives in the form of rewards can be incredibly powerful. But humans will almost always choose a smaller reward today over a bigger reward later. And, if a reward is too far into the future, guess what happens? People discount it altogether. As the saying goes, a bird in the hand is always worth two in the bush.

Let's go back to our carrot and stick metaphor. If you stick a tiny carrot at the opposite end of a field—hundreds of yards away—and try to direct a horse over to it, you're not going to have much luck. Even if you make it a huge carrot, the situation likely isn't going to change. It can be the biggest carrot that horse has ever seen (we're talking a freakishly huge carrot here), but that doesn't matter. It's so far off, the horse can barely see it. Plus, it'll take ages to walk all the way over there.

In this situation, you might give the horse a poke with your stick to get it to budge. The horse might move forward, too, and this could lead you to some false conclusions. Maybe sticks do work better than carrots after all. Maybe negative incentives are more powerful than positive ones.

This conclusion would be flawed, though. The problem isn't with positive incentives. It's with the way you're attempting to use them. Dangle a carrot right in front of the horse and allow it to take a nibble. Toss the carrot just a quick trot away, and the horse will rush straight to it. Keep tossing carrots out in front of you, and before you know it, you'll have moved the horse all the way across the field. Meanwhile, try prodding the horse in its behind for the next 500 yards... and you'll end up with a kick to the face. (If you're already applying this analogy to your own incentive programs, that's great. Save those ideas as we'll revisit this concept in tangible ways later.)

The bottom line here is this: Positive incentives are practically always superior to negative ones. But they must be implemented in the right way in order to be effective. That's why it's important to have a well-informed strategy when developing an incentive program for your business. (Which is also probably why you're reading this book).

Making Incentives Work for You

Working in the incentives industry, there's one thing that's become clear to us after several years of working with clients both large and small: No two clients are ever the same. That may seem obvious at first glance, but it's important to keep in mind. The same way that it can be difficult to predict what effect an incentive might have, it's also important to consider what the needs of your individual organization happen to be. At the end of the day, real world experience is the key to designing a corporate incentive program that has both the intended impact on your workforce, dealers or customers and aligns with the unique needs and values of your organization.

The takeaway here? As you continue through this book, keep thinking of *your ideal* incentive program, not some one-size-fits-all program that you found on Google. There's not a company in the world that couldn't benefit from a custom incentive program, if it is designed properly around its specific needs.

Increasing Engagement

At the end of the day, incentives are all about engagement. It doesn't matter whether you're talking about incentivizing employees or retaining customers: In both cases, you're looking to increase the target's engagement with your company.

The numbers are clear on this one. According to a study conducted by Gallup,[13] teams that actively work to increase engagement within their organization will see increases in both customer satisfaction and sales. These aren't small increases, either. On average, customer satisfaction increases by 10%, and sales numbers shoot up by 20%.

With numbers like these, it's shocking just how few companies really choose to focus on increasing engagement with their teams. Of course, the numbers make sense when you think about it. After all, wouldn't a properly engaged, focused, and dedicated workforce result in higher sales numbers and increased customer satisfaction?

Unfortunately, though, most companies tend to neglect or even completely overlook the importance of this aspect of their overall sales strategy. Marketing and product development are important, of course—but motivating your sales team is where you'll really trigger major jumps in revenue.

So, how do you increase engagement with your team? It's impossible for a large corporate organization to carry out daily engagement with, say, each individual service technician, parts manager, or HR employee. The sheer amount of labor and management involved would result in a negative return. It is possible, though, to put the necessary systems in place to ensure that this engagement happens on its own.

Those systems are ongoing incentive programs. These programs can be sales contests, dealership network spiff programs or customer rebate programs. But specifically, we're talking about programs that are separate from traditional salary or commission.

With the right incentives, your team can be valued, motivated, and successful. We already know that any form of increased engagement can result in a 20% jump in sales. Remember, though, salespeople are commission-motivated. Sales is often thankless, exhausting, draining work. People don't get into sales just because they enjoy the work. They pursue a career in sales because they're financially motivated.

Imagine the combined effect of increased engagement and financial incentives for your sales team. The sky's the limit.

Case Studies: Incentives as Game Changers

At this point, you might be thinking: Okay, sure, all of this sounds great. Incentives drive economic behavior. Increased organizational engagement, increased sales, I get it. But where's the proof that this will work for my organization?

Over the years we've worked with organizations across a number of industries to drive increases in sales, customer retention, and customer satisfaction. Let's take an (anonymous) look at how incentives can change the game.

One of our clients is in the auto industry. They came to us with a problem. Their product—the vehicles they're looking to sell—isn't actually being sold to the end user by a member of their sales team. Instead, their product makes its way from their inventory onto an auto lot at one of over 400 independent dealerships nationwide. This meant that literally thousands of individual salespeople were responsible for selling their vehicles to potential end users. The problem, though, was that they had no control over the preferences and pitches of those salespeople.

They needed to increase their market share of new, economy-priced vehicles at each and every one of these dealerships. The existing sales incentive, though, favored the sale of higher-priced vehicles. After all, a salesperson at an auto dealership who sells a car with a higher MSRP gets a commission based on that price. Why would they try to sell a cheap vehicle to a potential customer, when upselling them to a more expensive vehicle meant a bigger commission for them? This is an example of an existing incentive conflicting with the needs of a business.

What we needed to do was change the behavior of those salespeople. We had to figure out a way to incentivize them to sell a cheaper vehicle for less commission. In the end, we created a custom OEM incentive program that rewarded independent salespeople via reloadable debit cards for selling our client's lower-priced inventory.

The result? A year-over-year market share increase for the lower-priced vehicles while the program was in place. In year 1, the sales of incentivized units hit 1,165. At that time, our client's vehicle market share was 28%. The next year, the sales of incentivized units jumped to 4,220, a 362% increase. The vehicle market share for our client jumped, too, from 28% to 30.78% in this category. In year 3, sales of incentivized units increased to 5,379, with market share climbing all the way up to 35.05%. That's more than a 25% increase in existing market share from year 1 to year 3.

Just increasing sales isn't the only thing that incentives can do, though. In another client case study, our firm worked with a large *Fortune* 500 organization that was concerned about data collection inaccuracies. They had all of the systems in place to capture data properly at each step of their company's various departmental processes. The problem was worker behavior: Their administrative professionals just weren't submitting their monthly reports in a timely, structured, consistent way, and the stick, or penalties, weren't set high enough by certain managers to have meaningful impact.

To correct this behavioral issue, we created a stair-stepped incentive program. We worked to incentivize our client's administrative employees to file their reports on time, with rewards ranging from $10 - $40 per report depending upon frequency and timeliness. Now, $10 to $40 might not seem like a lot for sales professionals, but remember, these were the lower-paid administrative employees who weren't typically given the opportunity to earn extra cash. Many of these individuals ended up treating the incentives as lunch money, and just for doing their job, they essentially received a handful of free lunches per month (or at least the cash to purchase them).

The results of this program? The data speaks for itself. Monthly reporting increased by 360% year-over-year. The admins were thrilled with the extra cash. And the company was thrilled that their monthly dataset was finally complete.

Reward Options for Employee Incentives

Employee incentives can take different forms. A lot of companies make the mistake of simply handing out a cash bonus to an employee based on performance. While this can be effective to some degree, it simply can't match the impact that a personalized, branded debit card or engaging online portal has on your team.

Think about it: When you hand out a bonus check, your employee deposits it in the bank. Maybe they don't even get a physical check; it might just be a direct deposit that's added to their normal paycheck. Either way, those funds are immediately commingled with whatever is already in their account. By the end of the week (maybe even sooner), they've forgotten that the incentive they received is what's paying for their night out.

With a branded debit card, your company's logo is in front of your employee's eyes each and every time they go to spend a portion of their reward. They'll begin to subconsciously connect the behavior that led to the receipt of the incentive—for example, increased sales performance—with a pleasurable activity that they enjoy, such as a dinner at a fancy restaurant or a round of golf on the weekend. By making this subconscious connection, your employees will be even more inclined to repeat the positive behavior that you're looking for—whatever that behavior may be.

Reloadable debit cards aren't your only option, though. Another popular option is a customized, branded, secure, online merchandise portal. Employees receive their own login credentials and can log into their personal rewards account at any time to check on how many points they've accumulated. With points in hand (figuratively, at least), your organization's team members can shop for electronics, tools, sporting goods, and more.

If you're familiar with this sort of points system shopping from airline or credit card rewards, don't confuse those systems with what's possible, or what's recommended. We've actually found that the best practice is to make sure that point equivalents are designed to match with street pricing for the items on offer, unlike the inflated pricing typically associated with credit card or airline reward points systems.

Points-based programs can take multiple forms, too. You might pay out points based on individual sales numbers, with each employee receiving a personalized amount of points as they hit their goals. Or, you might reward an entire team with the same number of points per person once their group hits its quarterly sales goal. Some companies opt to mix things up with points matching, or even charitable points matching with an accompanying donation to a local organization. The sky's the limit when it comes to creative possibilities.

***

By now, you have some idea of what incentives are and how they work. As we've seen, incentives are at the core of human behavior. When it comes down to it, the answer to the question "why do we do the things that we do?" is surprisingly simple. It's the incentives!

But remember, incentives aren't limited to economic behavior. Moral incentives influence our choices as we differentiate between right and wrong, and social incentives have a major impact on how we navigate our relationships and interactions with the people in our lives.

Incentives can be complicated, just like human behavior. Predicting their efficacy can be a challenge, too. Sometimes they can have unintended effects, particularly if they're implemented in the wrong way. Plainly put, you don't want to go the route of the daycare businesses mentioned earlier.

It's all about taking the right approach to behavior modification. That's the subject of our next chapter.

Chapter 2

Behavior Modification

As we learned in the last chapter, incentives are at the core of our economic lives. Consider also that modern day humans are increasingly preoccupied with money, work, and the economy—whether it's the desire to save money here, earn more money there, make the right purchasing choice, choose the right investment, or whatever else. So it's easy to see just how important incentives are for you and your organization.

Now we're going to begin to shift our focus away from some of the more abstract topics that we covered in Chapter 1 and towards more practical and tangible concerns. Now that you have a high-level understanding of incentives, we can drill down and start to look into how your company can use them to achieve a variety of results.

First, it's important that we start to think about incentives in a certain way. Ensuring that the incentives you implement have the intended effect ultimately comes down to one thing: Taking the right approach to behavior modification.

Which raises a few key questions. How are incentives a question of behavior modification? How do caps and quotas impact progress? What's the "right reward" for your employees (the reward that will produce precisely the desired effect)? And, what can we learn from the working habits of New York City's cab drivers?

Incentives as Behavior Modification

At the end of the day, it's important to understand what exactly your organization is trying to accomplish with incentives.

It's easy to think about the end goal as a percentage increase in quarterly revenue, a fixed amount of added customer lifetime value, a higher customer retention rate, or something similar. There's nothing wrong with framing your goals in this way—so long as it's not the *only* way you think about them.

What do we mean? Essentially, you have to remember that, while your or your supervisor's end goal might be more sales or happier customers, focusing strictly on that goal will take your attention away from the path that gets you there. And that path is behavior modification.

The best way to think about the changes you're looking to make is to humanize them. Your organization is made up of a workforce, and that workforce is comprised of individual people. Those people exhibit specific behaviors each and every day on the job. Humans are creatures of habit,[14] and you can be sure that the behaviors you see in your workforce are habit- and pattern-based. Your goal with incentives shouldn't just be to make more money; it also should be to change the behaviors of your team members. It doesn't matter which department you're talking about, either. Let's look at a few examples.

First, think sales. Your initial goal might be a 10% increase in revenue. How do you make that happen? Walking into a meeting with your sales team and telling them to work harder probably isn't going to get you there. You have to understand what behaviors they're exhibiting, and how you can go about changing those behaviors. Are they consistently getting off to a slow start each quarter because they're worn out from pushing so hard at the end of the previous one? Incentivize something right out of the box in month one of Q1, Q2, Q3, and Q4. Are they slowing down towards the end of the quarter because they've already "hit their numbers?" (We'll discuss how to address this challenge of quotas and caps below.) Either way, you're not just trying to increase sales, your aim is to modify your team's behavior in a way that should produce that result.

The same thing goes for your human resources or customer service departments. Maybe there's something HR is doing (or isn't doing) during the hiring process, and you want to see it change. Or, maybe there are too many returns coming in through customer service that can't be restocked, and you want to change the way your team evaluates the feasibility of return with each customer. These examples may not be relevant to your business, but that doesn't matter. The point is that every business faces its own interdepartmental challenges, and the key to addressing them is through implementing incentives as a means of behavior modification.

Remember, too, that different employees are, well, different. Your sales team isn't your customer service team. In fact, you'll often find that certain personalities are drawn to specific roles within your organization. This is true across industries and niches. Salespeople are motivated by particular types of incentives that might be less appealing to someone in customer service, and vice versa. It may be that cash performance bonuses work well with your highly competitive and driven sales team, whereas your customer service department performs better when working together as a group towards a community giving goal. As long as you remember that you're looking to modify behaviors rather than simply "getting to the end goal" (of more sales, more customers, or whatever it might be), you'll be well on your way to implementing incentives in the best way possible.

Quotas and Caps: Enemies of Progress

Let's turn our attention to sales for a moment. More often than not, the clients we've worked with are focused on incentivizing their sales force. It's a common issue that companies run into: Their sales team is doing fine, but they need to take things up a notch. The problem is that they're not sure how. That's when they come to us.

Time and time again, we see our clients making the same mistake. It's understandable too: After all, conventional wisdom would dictate that they're doing the right thing.

Our experience proves otherwise, though. And, as we'll see below, scholarly research agrees with our assessment, too.

What are we talking about here? It's simple: caps and quotas.

We call them the enemies of progress.

Why? Because quotas and caps are practically guaranteed to stunt your company's growth.

We've seen it happen so many times with our clients. Their salespeople are on fire, and they're breaking one record after another. Things are looking up, and this quarter is bound to be the best in living memory. There's some kind of incentive structure in place—maybe just a simple cash commission—and a few key members of the sales team are raking in massive amounts of financial rewards.

But, there's a cap on how much they can earn per quarter. The cap is usually there because the company is concerned about paying out too much to any individual member of the sales team. Maybe their rationale is that they want everyone to perform well, rather than having a couple of superstars that get on a streak and rake in too much during a single quarter. Whatever the logic behind putting a cap on your sales team's rewards might be, we're here to tell you, the logic is flawed.

As soon as your star salesperson hits that cap, their streak is over. Maybe it's only a week before the numbers reset for the following quarter, but guess what? They've had the experience of hitting the cap. As a result, they now know that their earnings potential is limited. Come next quarter, why should they work their butt off week after week to exceed expectations? It makes more sense for them to lighten their workload a little and spread it out as evenly across the quarter as possible, because there's no advantage to hitting that cap early. They'll just be working long hours week after week, and they'll still have to do their job once the cap has been reached. They may actually put off closings until the next quarter.

The same goes for quotas. When there's a quota in place, your employees start to see that quota as their target. Their goal isn't to make as much as they can, or to sell as much as they can, it's to hit that minimum target. The target itself is arbitrary. You can set the quota high, but that won't have the effect you probably intend. Different sales people are different, and some of them simply won't be able to hit that quota. They'll feel discouraged early on in the quarter once they realize they don't stand a chance of hitting that goal, and it'll discourage them. Meanwhile, your superstar salespeople will reach the quota and then slow down. Why? Because they've hit their goal. Time to relax, right?

Whether it's quotas or caps, the issue here is psychological. When a cap or quota is achieved, the incentive dissolves. And if that cap or quota is unreachable, it's as if it never existed. When you start thinking about how your employees behave rather than simply focusing on the end results that you want, you can begin to see how important it is to shape their behavior. To illustrate this point further, let's turn to New York City and its fleet of cabs.

The Case of the Cabbies

Have you ever been to New York City on a rainy day? If you ask a New Yorker, they'll tell you it's practically written in stone: When you need a cab in the rain, you'll never find one. It's an immutable law of New York.

Let's think about that for a moment. Turning back to traditional, classical economics, this doesn't make any sense. According to the law of supply and demand, an increase in people looking for cabs (demand) should be met with an increase in the number of cab drivers (supply). Why is it that when there are so many people standing on the corner for a cab, the number of cabs seems to decrease?

A team of economists looked into this back in the late 1990s, and their findings had a big impact on the development of behavioral economics. Richard Camerer, George Loewenstein, Linda Babcock, and Richard H. Thaler found that cab drivers don't adhere to the logical, rational, unemotional law of supply and demand[15] in the way that classical economics would predict. No surprise there, though. After all: they're humans, and humans are emotional creatures with incentive-influenced behaviors.

Here's the thing: Cab drivers are trying to earn a specific amount of money each day. They have a quota in mind, whether that quota is set by the cab owner, or themselves if they're the owner. They're not out to earn as much as possible in their cab. Many drivers want to hit their quota and go home. On some days, they can hit their quota in a shorter amount of time. On other days, they'll work nearly twice as many hours before they reach their goal.

37

Why? The biggest determining factor is simply the number of people out and about looking for a cab ride. On some days, more people will opt to walk. As a result, there will be fewer people in need of a cab on any given street in New York. Cab drivers will then spend more time driving around, waiting to find their next passenger.

On a rainy day, the opposite happens. Everyone wants a cab, because they don't want to walk in the rain. As a result, it becomes incredibly easy for cab drivers to pick up one passenger after another, back to back. Camerer et al. found that once they've hit their quota early, they knock off for the day.

Why don't they just continue working? Why not earn more that day while the going is easy? Because they have a quota in mind. If there were no quota, they might keep working.

So-called income targeting can teach us a lot about what we *shouldn't* do if we want to incentivize employees properly. Don't set quotas. Don't set caps. Just create the right incentives, target them at the proper behaviors, and watch the sales roll in.

What's the Right Reward?

Assuming you don't put caps or quotas on your team, you're on your way to success when it comes to incentives. Before you reach your goals, though, there are other things to take into account.

One of the issues we've run into in the past with some of our clients involves the "right reward" for the right situation. Matching an incentive with a particular department, job, or product can seem like common sense. But things can get complicated quickly. If you don't provide the proper level of reward for a given scenario, you could end up with employees who are either totally unmotivated—or who are receiving a reward that's incommensurate with their experience and/or existing pay level. We want to avoid both of these outcomes, as neither of them is good for your bottom line in the long run.

Remember, the goal of any incentive is to change an employee's behavior. So, the big question becomes what kind of a reward is appropriate in order to bring about the correct change in behavior.

Let's look at a couple of examples. As we mentioned in the last chapter, one of our past clients is a vehicle manufacturer that works with independent dealerships nationwide. That client needed to incentivize independent salespeople at hundreds of dealerships to sell more of a specific economy vehicle, rather than trying to upsell their customers into something more expensive to earn a larger commission.

In this scenario, there are a couple of variables to consider. First, the target behavior we're looking to modify is a preference for which vehicle a given salesperson will attempt to talk a customer into buying. These salespeople generally have a tendency to upsell customers whenever possible, and we have to combat that existing behavior. The only way to do this is to ensure that the incentive we're offering makes it worth their while to change their habit and stop attempting to upsell customers. Simply put, that means doing our homework and making the incentive large enough to counterbalance the added commission that comes along with selling a more expensive vehicle.

Additionally, it might be worth making the incentive additive in order to encourage these salespeople to really zero in on selling the one particular vehicle. This could take on a number of forms, but a straightforward approach to this sort of incentivizing might involve setting extra bonus rewards at various levels of monthly sales. For example, a salesperson receives a fixed amount per vehicle sold, plus an extra fixed amount every time they sell five or more of those vehicles in a month.

Aside from needing to address the disparity between the commission on a cheaper vehicle and a more expensive one, something else to take into account when trying to set the right reward is the sheer value of the transaction itself. Let's assume that we're not even trying to incentivize a salesperson away from selling a more expensive vehicle and towards selling a cheaper one. Rather, let's say that we want them to sell our client's economy vehicle over a competing economy vehicle. In this case, their commission would be roughly the same either way.

That said, chances are good that we won't have much of an impact on behavior if we make our incentive a $10 reward for every $20,000 vehicle sold. Assuming the salesperson's commission is several hundred dollars or more, that $10 reward is a drop in the bucket.

On the flip side, though, a small incentive—such as $40 or $50—might have an incredibly dramatic impact on someone selling a lower-ticket item. If you offer a sales-person $50 for every $1,000 TV they sell, you're likely to have a major impact on their behavior. Closing the deal on a $1,000 TV isn't nearly as involved or time-consuming as convincing someone to buy a $20,000 car.

When determining the value of an incentive, it's also important to take into account the overall compensa-tion package of the employee. For example, consider the salesperson who regularly earns $100,000 or more per year. Incentivizing a particular sale with a $10 bonus will likely have a negligible effect on such a person. On the flip side, a small incentive for someone who's earning close to minimum wage could be a huge behavior modifier. For example, one of our clients provides small incentives as low as $1 for upselling customers on certain maintenance products. These salespeople earn just above minimum wage and, because these transactions are so plentiful, they can theoretically earn up to $5 extra per hour if they upsell each new customer. That's an incredible opportunity!

That said, it's also essential to consider how the incentive will fit into your bottom line overall. Chances are good that any given company will have far more employees and partners on the payroll who are earning close to minimum wage than those who are earning six figures. Incentivizing too many employees at the lower end of the pay scale— even with small incentives—can result in a relatively large expense for the company. Additionally, it could have a kind of boomerang effect further down the line once the incentive is removed or changed. If low-income employees have grown accustomed to increasing their wage with a particular incentive, they may resent it when that incentive eventually disappears.

For these reasons, it's incredibly important to find the sweet spot: An incentive that's perfectly matched to the department, the employee, that employee's salary, the behavior in question, and the desired outcome. Balancing this equation isn't always easy, but working with partners who can bring a lot of experience to the table definitely increases the likelihood of success.

Don't Let Your Ego Get In the Way

At this point, we've talked about two major pitfalls: Mistakenly placing caps and quotas on employees and failing to match the appropriate reward with the desired change in behavior. There's one other big mistake that we tend to see companies make, and it's an expensive one.

When we say expensive, we don't just mean figuratively. We mean literally. We've seen companies quickly lose market share when they do this, and recovering can end up costing them in lost time and lost revenue.

We're talking about ego.

To be frank, some companies let their ego get in the way and miss out on a ton of sales—and alienate customers.

Some companies are so convinced that their product is amazing—indispensable, even—that they laugh at the idea of incentivizing. Why do they need to incentivize their customers to buy? People will buy because the product is *just that good.* Why should they incentivize their sales team to sell more? Their team's already getting a commission, plus the product sells itself. Why do they need to worry about incentivizing HR, customer service, product development, or any other department? They know what they signed up for, they agreed to their salary, and besides, the product is going to fly off the shelves because people won't be able to live without it.

The other scenario that we've seen involves a new C-level executive coming onto the scene. As part of their initial review of company processes, they notice all the incentive programs in place —programs for their sales team, rebates for new customers, incentives for returning customers, bonuses for customer service... on and on. As part of a whole host of changes that they're looking to implement, they decide to wipe the slate clean. Who needs all these incentive programs, anyway? Don't people know that they're being paid a salary? Don't customers understand how good this product is, and how much they need it?

In no time flat, these companies lose market share. And the next thing you know, they're scrambling to put all of those incentives back in place.

What's the takeaway here?

If you've never put an incentive program in place, don't discount it out of hand. We assume you don't fall into this category if you're reading this book, but there's a good chance others in your organization don't necessarily agree with you on this. Some people have a tough time understanding just how effective incentives can be until they see them in action for themselves. As we said in Chapter 1, incentives are quite possibly the most powerful tool available for increasing revenue, expanding your market share, and attracting and retaining more customers.

If you have incentive programs in place, pull them at your own peril. There's nothing wrong with tweaking a program that's already working to make it better, of course. As we'll discuss below, making ongoing adjustments to an existing program is part of what it takes to be truly successful. But, don't let someone walk into the boardroom and pull the rug out from under all of your existing incentives. The consequences could be serious.

Staying Up To Date

So, you know that you need to avoid caps and quotas. You're going to be sure that your incentives are appropriate for the given department, employee, customer, and/or behavior that you're looking to modify. And, you know how dangerous it can be to discount incentives altogether, or to cancel existing programs that are working.

There's one more important thing to remember, though, when it comes to effectively modifying behavior. Everything that we've discussed so far can be thought of as essential to the initial lead up and execution of a solid incentive program. This last piece of advice is what you'll need to follow if you want to keep things running smoothly in the months and years to come.

Simply put, you've got to stay up to date. Incentives are just like any other part of your business. They can't be implemented and then put on autopilot indefinitely. Sure, some incentive programs can drive themselves for a while. But, eventually, you'll need to step in and make tweaks and updates as appropriate.

Think about it like this: Would you let your product development team kick up their feet on the desk because you have a successful product on the market? Of course not. Your competition is going to respond to whatever it is you've just released, and you can fully expect to lose market share if you don't continue to innovate.

Would you be comfortable with your marketing department continuing to "do what they've always done?" No way. In the age of digital marketing, what works this month might not work next month. You fully expect your marketing team to stay abreast of the latest developments in the marketing world, engaging your customers in a multidimensional way across every available platform.

In the same way, your incentive programs should be tweaked and updated on an ongoing basis. Never get too comfortable. If something's working, congratulations. That's a good thing. But you can't assume it's going to continue to work forever. In fact, you should assume by default that it *won't* continue working forever. In this day and age, nothing does. Things change in the blink of an eye, and your incentive program needs to be able to do the same.

On one level, this involves regularly re-evaluating both the success of your program, as well as how you're measuring that success. What are your KPIs (Key Performance

Indicators)? Are they in keeping with your goals? If your goals have shifted, the way that you measure success may need to shift, too.

Just as importantly, you must make sure your software is up to the task of adapting to changes in your program. When you're ready to implement something new into your current incentive program, is your software going to be able to respond? Or will you end up feeling hampered by technology that can't meet your needs? The last thing you want is to find yourself in a position where you must regularly switch platforms or providers whenever you want to make an adjustment in how and what you're incentivizing.

For these reasons, it's mission-critical that your incentive platform, including your software, processes and payment methods, remains agile enough to keep up with the changing times.

***

Incentives are aimed at behavior modification, plain and simple. You now should have a much clearer sense of exactly how to achieve the new behaviors that's you're looking for in your team. By avoiding caps and quotas, matching the right reward with the right scenario, keeping your ego in check, and staying up to date, you're well on your way to success.

With that in mind, it's time to turn our attention to the nitty gritty of an incentive program. In the next chapter, we'll take a look at the difference between employee rewards and employee recognition, and how to implement each in order to maximize your success.

Chapter 3

Employee Incentive Rewards Vs. Recognition Awards

In the last two chapters, we looked at what incentives are and how they relate to behavior modification. We started out with a high-level overview of human behavior in general, and then looked at the various ways incentives can have an impact on that behavior.

Now we'll start to drill down into what incentive programs actually look like for employers and organizations of various types and sizes. This is where the rubber meets the road.

If you're reading this book, you're probably in some sort of a leadership role at your company or organization. Maybe you're a small business owner, or a C-level executive. Maybe you're a department head or a sales manager.

Regardless of the specifics, there's one thing that holds true across the board: Managers, executives, and business owners all have a pretty good sense of how they want their department, organization, or company to operate.

You've got the experience necessary to understand the lived experience of a good portion of your department and/or company, and you have a sense of the different tasks and responsibilities that people are juggling. In a managerial or executive position, though, it can be easy to end up absorbed in the big picture and forget about all of the individual cogs working together to keep the machine functioning. Take a minute and picture all of those cogs, though. Think back to what it was like as an entry-level sales rep or customer support specialist.

Now, consider your co-workers in that position. Some of them probably did a better job than others. One sales rep would outperform another, or one customer service rep would take twice as many calls in a day as somebody else. Were these people gifted with otherworldly talents? Probably not. Sure, some people are better at sales than others, and one person might be more efficient on the phone than the next. But hard skills and soft skills alike can be learned. If someone wants to get good at something, they can.[16] It's not a question of innate talent, it's a matter of motivation.

That's the bottom line with any organization, no matter what sector it's in or how big it is. If a company's employees and channel partners are motivated, that company will excel. If its team is pessimistic, disinterested, and unmotivated, that company will struggle.

At this point, then, you might be wondering how to implement your first incentive program. In upcoming chapters, we'll move on to more complexity and specifics. First, though, we need to draw an important distinction between two types of incentives: *incentive rewards*, and *recognition awards*.

Incentive Rewards

On the surface, an incentive reward and a recognition reward sound pretty similar. In reality, though, the two are quite different. While they're intended to serve the same purpose—motivating your team to perform at an optimal level—they're implemented in different ways and can have vastly different effects.

Incentive rewards are an excellent way to change the behavior of your employees, and they're the primary focus of this book. As we've already discussed, incentives are at the bottom of much of human behavior. It doesn't matter whether you're talking about the economic, social, or moral aspects of human behavior, it all comes down to positive and negative incentives. And, as we've seen, positive incentives are generally much more effective than negative ones.

One of the best ways to offer positive incentives to your employees is through the implementation an employee rewards program. Multiple programs can run side by side in your organization, too. This can be especially useful for larger companies with a large number of teams and departments. As we'll see in later chapters, different types of incentive programs work better for certain departments.

There are all sorts of options available to you when it comes to setting up an incentive rewards program. At the end of the day, though, the big picture is pretty similar. Incentive rewards programs are intended as a form of bonus compensation, and that bonus compensation exists according to fixed rules. Under ideal conditions, everyone in your organization knows exactly what rewards are available to them and how to achieve those rewards — what benchmarks they'll need to hit to receive their bonus compensation. Employees then become intrinsically motivated to hit those goals, thanks to the reward structure. The goals and benchmarks can vary drastically from one department or company to another. The benchmarks for a sales department will likely look pretty different from those in a customer service department, for example.

For a rewards program to be effective, it's important for the rewards to be properly matched to the desired behavior. This is something we covered in Chapter 2, where we discussed what is and is not an appropriate reward level for a particular benchmark or goal. In addition to ensuring that rewards and behaviors are well matched, though, it's just as important for rewards to be fixed, clear, and consistent. When rewards are clearly communicated and easily distinguishable, they keep your team focused on future goals.

As we'll see shortly, employee *recognition* awards are quite different, and we'll talk about that it a bit. First, though, it's worth taking some time to outline the different kinds of rewards programs a company might put into practice. What exactly do rewards programs look like? What shape can they take?

Cash-Based vs. Points-based Rewards

Before we look at each type of reward option, there's a separate decision you'll need to make first: Do you want to offer your organization cash-based rewards, or use a points-based rewards system to keep them motivated?

One of the biggest advantages of a cash-based system is simplicity. Incentivizing employees with cash can be as easy as setting thresholds for achievement and cutting some checks. For small businesses with very limited incentives needs, a cash-based program might make the most sense.

That said, there are a lot of advantages to a points-based system, and it's what we often recommend to our clients.

A points-based system doesn't necessarily mean that you must offer merchandise rebates through an online portal or something similar. Points can simply be redeemed for cash, which is almost as simple as a straight cash-based system. Even under these circumstances, though, points offer several advantages.

For one thing, there's something intangible but markedly different about how it "feels" to receive a points-based reward. Your employees already get a paycheck, right? And in the case of your sales team, they're likely already receiving commission checks based on their sales performance each quarter. Particularly in the latter case, simply adding on another cash incentive on top of existing commissions can sometimes have a negative effect. It muddies the waters, and employees can end up confused about the difference between their existing commission and this "new incentive program" that "somebody up in corporate" has decided to introduce. How exactly is this different from the commission checks they already get?

A points-based reward system gives employees the impression that they are getting something above and beyond a commission. Sure, they might just be switching those points out for cash straight away, but the act of receiving the points and then "cashing them in" via an online portal can help set the experience apart from their standard bi-weekly pay or quarterly bonus.

Lastly, points help to foster healthy competition. Depending on your company culture, people might not feel comfortable comparing their relative achievements in terms of dollars. Your sales superstar may be proud of what they've accomplished (and happy about the balance in their checking account), but they probably wouldn't drop a dollar figure over a casual lunch conversation. With points, though, this taboo is removed. Of course, everyone knows what points are equivalent to. But this is one of those quirks of human behavior that you can use to your advantage. Employees will be much more likely to brag about their points achievements, which can make high-level rewards appear more within reach for employees who are struggling to keep up. If my buddy two cubicles down can do it, so can I, right?

Once you've decided whether you want to go with a cash-based or points-based system, you'll need to choose how the points are distributed. We'll be discussing each of these options in greater detail in future chapters. But, for now, let's just look briefly at each.

Prepaid Branded Debit Cards

Whether you're using a points-based or cash-based system, one of the easiest ways to pay out rewards to employees is via a prepaid branded debit card.

You might wonder what advantage this has over simply cutting a check. That would be cheaper, faster, and easier, wouldn't it? There's nothing wrong with rewarding an employee with a check. But prepaid branded debit cards carry with them all sorts of benefits.

One major advantage of using a branded debit card is the "branded" component. Depending on how your company handles its payroll and accounting, you may not even issue physical checks. If you also pay out rewards directly with cash, all an employee will ever see is a bank deposit. Within days, that money will have been commingled with their existing funds to a point where it's no longer recognizable.

This doesn't mean your employee or channel partner won't still be happy about the reward. But it does mean that the shelf life of that feeling is pretty limited, and the odds of them holding it in their mind's eye as a continued motivating factor at work are fairly low.

With a prepaid branded debit card, things change. Employees will use the card many times over the course of weeks or months. Each time they pull it out of their purse or wallet, they'll be reminded of the reward itself and the behaviors associated with the reward (higher sales, better customer satisfaction, or whatever the case may be). They'll grow to associate that modified behavior with the pleasure that comes as they make purchases.

Setting up a prepaid branded debit card rewards system is easier than you might think. In its simplest form, you can order cards in bulk, and simply hand them out as needed. However you implement them, the brand affinity from your logo constantly appearing in front of your recipients is hard to beat.

Reloadable Branded Debit Cards

A reloadable branded debit card works in much the same way as a prepaid one, but is reusable. A prepaid card is a one-and-done sort of reward. Once the balance is spent, your recipient will toss the card and won't be able to use it again. With a reloadable card, you can top off the balance every time an employee hits a certain benchmark.

You'll save money because you'll need fewer cards, and reloadable cards can be personalized with an employee's name. In this sense, the reloadable card is more of a personal, customizable gift than a prepaid debit card.

Virtual Debit Cards

Both of the previous card options have the advantage of being tangible. You can actually place them in the hands of a recipient, look them in the eye, and thank them for their hard work. The connection this creates can be highly effective for further incentivizing the new behavior you're encouraging the employee to develop. And as we've already mentioned, having a physical, branded card in their possession will remind them of the connection between their behavior, the incentive they've received, and your company. This effect will occur each and every time they use the card.

But consider for a moment how common online shopping has become, with 80% of Americans now shopping online.[17] Some people cite added selection as their primary motivation for going online instead of heading to a local store. But, more often than not, people are shopping online for one simple reason: It's more convenient.

When you're shopping in a retail store or having a meal at a restaurant, pulling out a physical card when the bill arrives is par for the course. But when shopping online, most people have their credit card information already stored in their computer. They'll enter it once, and their browser will autofill the information whenever they go to make a future purchase.

So it's easy to see how some recipients may not end up handling the physical card that you give them on a regular basis if they're making most of their purchases online. Thus, a virtual debit card can be a viable alternative to a standard, tangible card.

You may have already had and used a virtual debit card. If you're not familiar with them, though, they're exactly what they sound like. Rather than possessing an actual physical card, a virtual debit card is simply a collection of the same information contained in a standard card. Typically, the recipient is emailed a copy of the card information, including the number, the expiration, and a security code. It's even possible to pay with a virtual debit card in person, depending on the store. Some retail outlets will honor a virtual card, allowing you to show them an image of the card and virtually "scan" it at checkout.

Why go with a virtual card over a physical one? Apart from the convenience, virtual debit cards are cheaper to implement. There's no physical card to order, print and send, thus reducing overhead costs, and issuing them is faster and easier. If you're running a large organization with hundreds or even thousands of employees, hand delivering—or even mailing out—hundreds of physical cards isn't just expensive, it's also time-consuming. With virtual debit cards, you can issue rewards to your employees instantly. Refilling the card is fast and easy, too. Plus, virtual debit cards pair well with points-based online portals. Once an employee exchanges the points they've accumulated for cash, they can use their virtual debit card instantly to make a purchase using the portal.

An important note: We've found that most organizations opt for a physical prepaid or reloadable card because the tangible feeling of your brand in the recipient's hand is unmatched. There isn't a right or wrong choice; we're simply illustrating the continuing popularity of physical cards even in the age of the iPhone.

Recognition Awards

Incentive rewards have many advantages for incentivizing changes in employee behavior, but they're not the only way to do so. *Recognition awards* are another option. At first glance, it's easy to confuse the two and not just because they sound similar. They both reward employees and channel partners for a job well done, and they both assist in effective behavior modification. But they are surprisingly different in terms of implementation and potential effects.

Employee *incentive* rewards are highly specific. They're typically tied to a particular activity—such as selling an item—and are often replicable over time. For example, a company selling shoes might decide to run an incentive program for their salespeople. To sell a particular model of shoes during the holiday rush, they offer a $10 reward for every pair sold. This type of an incentive reward is open to every single salesperson, and there's every reason to believe that dozens (if not hundreds) of salespeople will each receive at least some level of reward.

Recognition awards are actually the opposite of this scenario, at least in some ways. For one thing, recognition usually involves actual competition. Sure, it's possible for employees to get competitive with an incentive rewards program like the one mentioned above. A little friendly competition can be helpful, as your team members can synergistically encourage one another to increase their level of performance during the period of time that the rewards program is in place.

With recognition awards, though, the competition is much more overt. Whereas the number of incentive rewards recipients is essentially unlimited, employee recognition awards are usually only handed out to a small number of participants. Imagine a sales force dealing with much more expensive items than shoes, such as the sales team at a car dealership. In advance of their slowest quarter of the year, the dealership announces an employee competition: The top three employees who manage to sell the most cars by the end of the quarter will receive an all-expense-paid trip to Aruba. An employee finishing in fourth place won't receive anything at all, even if they're only one sale and a handful of dollars away from finishing in third place.

Remember our discussion of the unintended consequences of certain incentives back in chapter one? Incentives are the best way to modify behavior—but they can also have surprising repercussions.

Consider for a moment the effect this awards-based competition will have on the sales team. Initially, everyone will probably be excited about the chance to win a trip to Aruba. Competition may be fierce. Depending on the dynamics within the sales team, this kind of a competition could actually lead to a lack of cooperation between team members.

Assuming that doesn't happen, though, another potentially unintended consequence is likely to arise later on during the quarter. At the beginning of the competition, everyone will have a more or less equal shot of winning one of the three trip packages. As the weeks wear on, though, the number of people who are legitimately in the running will dwindle. Imagine a sales team of 50+ representatives spread across several locations. During week one, every rep has more or less the same number of sales. By week seven or eight of the quarter, a handful of star salespeople will have likely pulled ahead by some margin. There might be six or seven employees with fairly similar sales numbers, all still in the running to win the trip. The other 40+ members of the team are so far behind that it's highly unlikely they'll be able to bridge the gap in the final weeks of the quarter.

So, what happens? The handful of employees at the top will likely work even harder. The salespeople in the top three positions will all have their noses to the grindstone, doing their best to stay in the lead. Meanwhile, the people in positions four, five, six, and so on will be pushing themselves to make enough extra sales to pull ahead and win one of the trips.

But what about the other 40 or so reps? They are so far from being in the top three positions that they completely give up on winning the trip. While this could be innocuous, it can also actually demotivate a large chunk of your sales team. They begin to develop antipathy to the competition, and maybe even to the sales process (at least until the competition is over).

Combining Incentive Rewards and Recognition Awards

So, what's the takeaway here? Are incentive rewards just qualitatively better than recognition awards? Should you kick recognition awards to the curb in place of a strictly rewards-based program, one with an unlimited number of recipients, and no ceiling apart from the one enforced by limited inventory?

Not necessarily. While it is important to consider the potentially unintended consequences of a recognition competition like the one mentioned above, you don't have to throw the baby out with the bath water. One of the best ways to mitigate these sorts of potentially negative consequences is by simply combining both types of incentive programs into one seamless, diversified offering for your employees.

Imagine offering some combination of the above offerings. The three Aruba trips are still on the line for your top salespeople, sure. But everyone selling a particular model of car (perhaps one that you have way too much inventory of right now) will also get an extra $100 added to their reloadable branded company debit card, in addition to the standard commission for that model.

Late in the quarter, your best salespeople will still kick things up a notch as they vie for one of the top three spots, but the rest of your sales team will have their own reason to keep their sales efforts in high gear. They'll continue to push that particular model to rack up a few more $100 bonuses before the quarter ends.

Running incentive and rewards programs simultaneously can have other positive effects. Consider one of the other biggest differences between the two. With an awards program, your employees are competing over a long period of time—a quarter, or perhaps even an entire year—for a payoff at the end. For some people, this kind of incentive works great. They're able to stay focused on the long-term end goal, and that's motivation enough for them.

But for most people, instant gratification is much more compelling than some distant award. In his book *Carrots and Sticks*, Ian Ayres[18] found that most people are more than willing to give up a huge reward for a much smaller one. The condition? The huge reward is far into the future, and the much smaller one is instant. So long as people have to wait for what they perceive to be a long time to get a big reward, most will consistently choose something comparatively tiny—so long as they can have it immediately.

You can use this tendency to your advantage when implementing an incentive program. While some employees (including your top salespeople) are focused on the long-term goal of the Aruba trip, the rest of your team receives an instant reward every time they sell a particular model of car. Incentive rewards are ongoing: They're happening every single minute of every day. Anytime an employee manages to sell one of the cars in question, they're rewarded. It doesn't get much more immediate than that. And, of course, the salespeople who have a real shot at winning the award will still benefit from receiving this instant reward, too. And best of all, both of these programs can run seamlessly in one portal, making the process incredibly simple for management and participants.

**

At this point, you're probably itching to implement an incentive program of your own because you know they're the best way to modify employee behavior, and you're ready for that 30% year-over-year revenue increase.

But before you launch your first incentive program, you'll want to crunch some numbers, and you have to understand how to calculate the program's Return On Investment (ROI). We'll get to that next..

Chapter 4

Calculating ROI for Incentive Programs

It doesn't matter what aspect of your business or organization you're talking about. Whether it's sales, customer service, product development, or any other aspect of your company, one question takes precedence over all others: What's the ROI?

Calculating ROI is essential to measuring success. If you're a C-level executive or business owner, you want to know exactly how the decisions you're making are impacting your bottom line. As a departmental manager, it's important to keep track of how your employees' activities contribute to (or fail to contribute to) overall profitability. And if you're a salesperson or other company employee, it's safe to assume that the easiest way to move up the food chain is to demonstrate the ROI of your work to the powers that be.

With our clients, we often point to year-over-year proportional improvements in returns as an indicator of an incentive program's success. As any savvy executive or business owner knows, though, returns alone don't tell the whole story. Costs are just as important, and you need to take them into account when determining return on investment for any program you implement. This raises some important questions:

- How does the ROI of an incentive program compare to other forms of marketing and sales promotion?

- Are there cost advantages associated with incentives that make them superior to other promotional activities?

In this chapter, we'll take a look at some common marketing and sales techniques and see how they measure up to a carefully implemented incentive program so you'll have a good sense of how you can expect an incentive program to perform comparatively.

Traditional Advertising

John Wanamaker, the early 20th century advertising pioneer, famously said: "Half of the money I spend on advertising is wasted. The trouble is, I don't know which half." If you've ever tried to run a full-scale traditional advertising campaign, you know exactly what he meant.

Attempting to calculate the return on investment for a traditional ad campaign often seems impossible. Sure, you can come up with a figure that represents how much your total ad spend will be, but trying to determine how much of that advertising leads to actual sales and revenue increases is a bit of a guessing game. Are new sales due to the direct-response TV ads you ran? Are they coming from awareness magazine advertising, or community-based initiatives on public radio? If you run a multi-faceted ad campaign, what portion of new sales are coming from each individual medium?

It's possible to do some focus group research to determine your ads' effectiveness on certain segments of the population, but this data still won't give you much in the way of exact numbers when it comes to actual sales and revenue. Plus, trying to do this sort of research adds a new cost layer to an already expensive proposition. And while many firms use dedicated toll-free numbers and URL's specific to certain ad campaigns, that type of tracking isn't foolproof either.

Consider these numbers:[19] On average, a national 30-second TV spot costs upwards of $300,000, and the top end during a major event could cost $8 million. Once. That's right, we're not talking about something that you'll put in front of consumers half a dozen times in an hour. This is a 30-second spot, appearing once. If you know anything about advertising, you know that once is as good as "not at all." An ad in a national magazine could cost $250,000. Full-page ads in national newspapers sometimes go for over $1 million.

Depending on your industry, and especially if you're in a business-to-business enterprise, you might be inclined to insert ads into trade magazines. That's fine, but ask yourself something: Are you actually still reading those magazines? When was the last time you saw an ad for something in a trade magazine and made a purchasing decision because of it? At best, this advertising does little more than improve your name recognition. At worst, it's a complete waste of valuable resources.

Don't get us wrong, traditional advertising can still be an important part of a robust marketing strategy, particularly if you're a large organization. But attempting to measure the ROI from a traditional ad campaign is very difficult to do (if not impossible). If you're looking for a 20% or more year-over-year revenue increase, running a magazine ad probably isn't the best way to get you there.

Direct Mail

Direct mail offers enables you to measure return on investment more accurately. To be fair, some of your customers may make an additional purchase due to the subliminal effects of direct mail and increased name recognition, and measuring those purchases isn't something you can easily do. However, including a promotional code on a piece of direct mail allows you draw a direct correlation between your ad spend and the number of leads who actually follow through with a purchase. Whether you're a car dealership sending out a local promo flyer or an online retailer offering a coupon code for first-time buyers, determining ROI from direct mail is certainly more doable than, say, a television ad.

But it's important to be realistic about just how expensive direct mail can be. The cost of postage continues to rise— something that we're all reminded of every time we need to send our annual holiday cards. Sending out thousands of mailers can get expensive in a hurry and, much like television, radio, print, and other traditional advertising, you run the risk of spending tens of thousands of dollars on a campaign... and never seeing a single sale. This sort of thing happens more often than you might think. A poorly targeted direct mail piece can turn into an enormous waste of valuable marketing funds.

To sum up, direct mail does indeed have its place. In the right industry at the right time—and with the right customers, and the right message—direct mail can be effective. If your organization is large enough, direct mail might play a valuable role as part of a larger marketing campaign. In general, though, it's an expensive (and sometimes risky) way of attempting to increase revenue.

Digital Marketing

Twenty years ago—even a decade ago—many businesses had little to no digital presence. The whole notion of needing to market your business online was something that many small- to medium-sized businesses (SMBs) simply opted to forego. Digital marketing was seen as something that huge companies with big budgets could dedicate both money and employee time to. As a smaller business, you might do this sort of stuff if you had some extra time. Maybe you'd post on social media occasionally or make the occasional website update (one blog post per year, anyone?).

Those days are gone and digital marketing is no longer optional. Virtually every company of every size needs a digital presence these days. If you're running a business, you need to market your organization digitally.

Things are far from rosy in the world of digital marketing, though. When we talk about digital marketing, we're usually referring to four separate arenas: Paid traffic, including both pay-per-click search ads and display remarketing, search engine optimization (SEO) for organic traffic, email marketing, and social media. Let's take a look at each of these in turn.

Paid Traffic

Many organizations get excited about the idea of paid traffic and it's easy to understand why. After all, the idea of measuring ROI with paid traffic is essentially built into the medium itself. If you're using something like Google AdWords to run paid search or display ads (the latter of which are often called "retargeting ads," as they pop up to remind you of a website you recently visited), you can track visitor behavior from the time they click on an ad to the moment they make a purchase. This holds a lot of appeal, especially against traditional forms of advertising like television, radio, magazines, and so on.

Unsurprisingly, paid traffic can be expensive: Something like 95% of Google's revenue[20] is derived from its paid advertising fees. Large businesses regularly spend upwards of $50 million per year[21] on AdWords campaigns, and even small businesses can spend $9,000 to $10,000 a month on average. That's over $100,000 per year in ad spend.

Paid traffic isn't just costly because of the fees assessed by Google, either. Particularly if you're a larger organization, running an effective AdWords campaign means connecting with a trained professional who can bring paid search expertise to the table. Believe us, you don't want to throw $10,000 or more per month at AdWords if you're not familiar with the platform. But these services also add costs to the equation.

This leads us to another downside of paid traffic. While it is indeed much easier to calculate ROI from paid search and retargeting campaigns than from other forms of advertising, there's no guarantee that a click is going to turn into a sale or conversion. Any analysis of AdWords involves measuring both click-through rate (CTR) and conversion rate, because most of the clicks you receive won't actually result in conversions. The downside is that it's possible to spend many, many thousands of dollars on an AdWords campaign...and end up without a single sale or conversion.

The bottom line is this: Paid traffic can be effective, and it's worth including search and retargeting ads as part of your overall digital strategy. But as this form of advertising becomes increasingly competitive and more costly by the day, it's also becoming less attractive for many businesses and industries.

Search Engine Optimization (SEO)

Search engine optimization (SEO) is an umbrella term used to refer to all of the individual marketing actions that collectively contribute to better search rankings for your website. If you're writing a blog, you're working on SEO. If you're making small but purposeful changes to meta tags on one of your website's pages, you're doing SEO. And if you're trying to build backlinks to your website, you're also doing SEO.

If you've been in the digital world long enough, you probably remember the good old days of SEO a decade ago, when Google's search algorithm was significantly less sophisticated. Today, there's no quick and simple way to trick Google into giving your site a first-page ranking. Google's algorithm is far too sophisticated to be suckered into bumping your page up without good reason. The only way to end up at the top of search results is by building a robust, informative, user-friendly website that Google perceives as both helpful for users and highly authoritative in its particular industry or niche. This isn't something that you can achieve overnight, it takes a lot of time, money, and resources.

Making significant improvements with SEO involves hiring a professional. If your organization is large enough to employ full-time digital marketers, you may have someone on staff who handles this. Otherwise, you'll need to outsource this work and the nature of SEO calls for ongoing work. You need to publish new content every week or two, and regularly update your site to ensure that it looks, feels, and reads as current and authoritative. One blog post every month isn't going to cut it. Content is king in the world of SEO and digital marketing these days. The more useful, informative content your organization publishes, the better it will perform in terms of search engine ranking. A site that fails to answer common customer questions and provide a user-friendly experience simply won't rank on page one of search results in the vast majority of cases. This all costs real money.

One of the biggest challenges with organic SEO is measuring ROI. A few years ago, it was easier to see exactly what searches were leading to organic traffic using a platform like Google Analytics. You could see which search phrases and keywords were resulting in sales, versus which keyword phrases led to a user bouncing (click back) from your site after 5 or 10 seconds. Now, though, Google Analytics has removed much of this capability. This means that while you can measure overall organic traffic and the number of conversions stemming from it, it's very difficult to tell which search terms are actually resulting in sales. As a result, you have to put resources into SEO for a wide variety of keywords and search phrases—some which may not actually be earning your business any revenue.

There's no question: SEO isn't optional if you rely on your website for leads or sales. Maintaining high organic search presence is essential to the success of any business in the modern digital era. But, measuring ROI with SEO is very difficult—and keeping your site at the top of search results is far from cheap (or easy).

Email Marketing

Alongside paid ads and SEO, email marketing is another common component of a comprehensive digital marketing strategy. Years ago, most SMBs would only bother with sending out the occasional email —maybe a monthly newsletter (which half the time someone would forget to write). Or, if they were a B2B company, they'd send out the occasional new product notification email to some of their accounts. Overall, though, email was used primarily as a direct communication tool.

In many ways, email continues to be a direct communication tool—but of a different flavor. Email marketing today arguably has become one of the most commonly used (and some would argue most effective) forms of direct marketing. Companies both large and small use email to communicate directly with their customers. Even very small businesses have sophisticated email automations in place to trigger workflows and sequences based on customer behavior. Did you leave an item in your online shopping cart? You'll get an email notification reminding you to complete the transaction. Click through a specific link in a previous email? That click triggers a specific workflow, causing you to receive a new string of emails based on your past behavior.

In terms of sheer customer reach,[22] email beats other forms of digital marketing hands down. Roughly 3 billion people worldwide use email on a regular basis. Proponents of email marketing will argue that it offers significantly better ROI than paid search ads, social media, or virtually any other form of digital advertising.

On the flip side, though, there's also a lot of background noise in the email marketing world. It's widely estimated that there are over 250-billion email messages sent every day around the world. Meanwhile, the average office worker receives around 121 emails each day[23]—and that number is rising, too.

Take a moment to consider what your inbox looks like right now. How many of the emails you receive each day end up being read? How many are deleted without a second thought? If you use Gmail, most sales emails likely end up in your "Promotions" tab. It's not uncommon for the open rates of emails in this tab to be abysmally low.

Some marketers are beginning to wonder how much longer it will be before people begin to tune out sales emails completely. Even as recently as a few years ago, only the largest companies were using automation. Now, with virtually every business sending a slew of emails on a regular basis, it might only be a matter of time before email marketing completely loses its effectiveness.

Email marketing is also becoming more difficult in the wake of the new EU General Data Protection Regulation (GDPR). Under GDPR, sending so-called "cold emails" could result in a violation. Depending on the severity of a violation, a company could be fined anywhere from €10 - €20 million, or 2-4% of annual global revenue—whichever is greater. Where it was common practice in the past for companies to scrape together lists of potential contacts (particularly in the B2B arena) and send out cold emails, this practice is more dangerous and unscrupulous than ever. Meanwhile, building a high-quality, valuable, effective list of warm email contacts is something that takes a massive amount of time and resources. There's no shortcut to putting together such a mailing list.

In the end, email marketing is another box that you'll need to check as part of your company's overall approach to meeting sales and revenue goals via digital means. But it's far from perfect, and ROI may not measure up to some of the claims that email marketers regularly make about the medium.

Social Media Marketing

Ah, social media. In our experience, there are three types of social media users in the business world (and the same goes for social media use outside of the business realm). First, you have those who are practically hooked on social media. They're always chatting you up about the latest update to this or that platform, or a new feature that they just can't get enough of. You see them posting on social media more times per day than you pull your phone out of your pocket. Next, you've got people who either use social media because it's a practical way to keep up with goings on around the office and in the industry, or who begrudgingly engage in social media out of sheer necessity. Finally, there are those who can't stand social media and ignore it completely.

If you fall into the first group, you're likely chomping at the bit to exploit social media to its fullest capacity as part of your organization's digital marketing strategy. You might be convinced that you don't need a social media manager or outside marketing agency to handle such things. After all, you're on social media all the time, and you can take care of managing an account. If you're one of those people who uses social media for the sake of practicality—you're much less likely to think of social media as essential to your company's online presence. And if you can't stand social media, you probably think it's all pointless and just something "the kids are into." Whatever your stance, social media is constantly changing, and the ROI story isn't getting any better.

As recently as five years ago, "social media marketing" was all the rage. Marketers were convinced that it was the wave of the future. A lot of people went so far as to ditch email, and some even decided to more or less ignore the responsibility of updating their website in favor of pouring extra time and energy into their Facebook page. For a while, things looked good for social media. Everything your company posted to its Facebook company page—100% of new content—would show up in followers' feeds. Plus, the amount of background noise was still relatively low: You weren't yet competing with every other business in your niche for bandwidth.

Now, things are completely different. A few years back, social media platforms instituted a slew of changes to the way their business pages work. One of the most impactful changes was the way that posts appear in followers' feeds. Now, it's unlikely that the majority of your posts and updates will actually show up in the feeds of your followers. Instead, only those posts that start to gain a lot of traction—meaning, the posts that already have a lot of shares, likes, and views—will gain enough momentum to actually make it in front of the majority of your followers. How do you start to gain that traction, you ask? By promoting (or boosting) the post. In many ways, then, business pages on social media have turned into a pay-to-play system, where you have to shell out a chunk of change to promote any post that you actually want your followers to see.

Combined with the normal paid social media ad budget, this has made social media increasingly expensive. What was previously a free digital marketing medium that an existing employee could update in their spare time has turned into an expensive, cumbersome, time-consuming endeavor that requires dedicated management. Think about just how many new items show up in your feed each and every day, whether it be on Facebook, Twitter, Instagram or any other social media platform. How many of them do you actually read? How many do you even end up scrolling through, much less clicking on?

As the costs of social media have gone up, ROI has naturally gone down. While you're afforded some of the same advantages as paid search ads when it comes to calculating ROI (meaning, you're able to track user click-through and purchase behavior), the actual return itself can be a bit of a letdown. Overall, maintaining a social media presence is definitely something your organization needs to do— but don't expect the ROI to blow your socks off the way it would have a few years ago.

Sales and Discounts

Virtually every business at one time or another uses sales and discounts to generate revenue growth. If you're a B2C company, running seasonal sales and theme-driven promotions isn't really optional; it's something every other company in your niche likely does, and you'll have to do it, too. Even if you're an organization in the B2B space, you might find that some sort of discount or other promotional offer can be an effective way to close new leads.

There's no question that discounts can work. They've been around in their current form since at least 1887,[24] when Coca-Cola distributed the first ever modern coupon. And to be sure, there's some pretty clear science behind how and why coupons work. Dr. Paul J. Zak of Claremont Graduate University conducted a study[25] which demonstrated that coupons are capable of both raising oxytocin levels in recipients and reducing rates of respiration and sweating. In other words, coupons calm you down and make you feel good.

That said, there are downsides to running sales promotions and discounts. In many instances, aggressively discounting your products can create a "race to the bottom" scenario. This is precisely what's happened to the grocery industry[26] in recent years—an industry now seeing less than 1% annual growth struggling to stay afloat in terms of profit margins. According to some analyses, the persistent and widespread discounting that's caught on as a kind of industry norm across grocery stores is largely to blame for stunted sales, poor growth, and low profit levels.

Once consumers come to expect a certain type of retailer (or even an entire industry) to offer discounts all the time on a wide variety of their products, the effectiveness of the discounts becomes negligible. Rather than actually bringing in new customers the way a properly designed promotion ought to, this sort of discounting does nothing more than reduce an organization's autonomy and brand image. In consumers' minds, your brand becomes associated with constant discounting. And if you don't deliver, consumers will shop elsewhere.

Over time, excessive sales and discounts can tarnish your brand's image. This is especially problematic if you've built up a brand that consumers think of as "premium." Perhaps your customers are willing to pay a slightly higher price for the quality, features, and even the image that your brand offers. If you begin to aggressively discount your products, you lose this premium space in your customers' minds almost by definition. This can create a brief burst of revenue as consumers rush to get a great deal on a premium brand, but your products will eventually lose their luster in the marketplace and come to be seen as a low dollar, discount product. Generally speaking, that's the last thing you want.

Although sales and promotions can definitely move the needle, organizations need to be cautious when attempting to implement them, and avoid over-reliance that can have unintended (and negative) consequences.

Incentive Program ROI

We've now considered traditional, digital and social marketing and virtually all these approaches to generating revenue and driving sales have some role to play in the trajectory of your organization. But, in our experience, none can compare to the virtually guaranteed results and excellent return on investment that comes with a properly-implemented incentive program.

Consider all the advantages that an incentive program offers as compared to, say, a traditional advertising campaign. Where the cost of traditional advertising and direct mail continues to rise, the fees associated with implementing an incentive program have actually *decreased* in recent years due to improvements in efficiency and availability of associated technologies. Putting together a turnkey, customized online portal is simpler than ever and it's no longer something that requires the kind of massive investment that only the largest companies can afford to make.

When compared to digital marketing, incentive programs still win out in terms of ROI. Recall that while SEO is important, measuring its ROI directly is next to impossible. And while paid traffic can result in a lot of dead-end leads as potential customers click through without purchasing, effectively running up a large AdWords bill with no actual return on your investment, incentives produce a return by definition on every dollar spent. Also recall how crowded the social media space has become. Intra-organizational incentive programs don't suffer from this sort of shortcoming, as it's up to you how many and what types of programs your company will offer.

While discounts and sales promotions offer certain advantages that other types of marketing can't, we saw above just how dangerous they can be when used excessively. Incentives provide a much safer and wider-reaching means of boosting sales, without the risks associated with coupons and discounts.

On top of these advantages, we're also beginning to see significantly more competition between banks that provide these sorts of services. A few years ago, your options for a service provider were fairly limited, but there are now all sorts of options in the marketplace. As a result, banks are being forced to offer more reasonable rates for reloadable debit cards, virtual debit cards, and the other services associated with a comprehensive incentive program. The upshot of this is that incentive programs have never been more affordable for organizations of all sizes. Even a startup with a very small sales team could reasonably look to implement an incentive program, considering how low the costs can actually be.

Calculating ROI for Incentive Programs: Efficiency and Returns

As mentioned above, certain forms of marketing—such as paid traffic or print advertising, for example—can involve large expenditures with sometimes zero return on investment. Whether it's an ad in a trade magazine that practically no one ever sees or responds to, or a Google AdWords campaign that runs up a $5,000 bill on click-throughs that never turn into actual sales, many of the marketing tactics mentioned above—including both traditional and digital approaches—can be dangerously unprofitable.

Whether it's an internal sales spiff program or an external customer rebate program, one of the best things about a properly implemented incentive programs is its total immunity to this sort of problem. Consider for a moment how one type of incentive program might work, as described in Chapter 3. An announcement is made to your sales team regarding a particular product. You need to move more of this product in the coming months, as you currently have an overstock—and the season for this product will be over by the end of next quarter. You let your team know that they can expect to receive an incentive reward of $50 on their reloadable debit card for each of these items that they sell, in addition to their standard salary and commission.

Every time this product sells, you'll be paying out an additional $50 for that sale. You know this in advance. Undoubtedly, you've set this amount at the proper threshold: not so low that it fails to properly incentivize behavior (as a $10 incentive might fail to persuade a high-paid salesperson), but not so high as to seriously cut into your profit margin.

You can calculate this cost ahead of time and determine what makes sense for your organization. How badly do you want to move this particular product? How much do you want to increase revenue over the next quarter? Once you do the math on the total amount that you could expect to pay out in incentives compensation, you know ahead of time what the overall cost of a particular campaign might be. There's no guesswork involved. Rather than crossing your fingers that an AdWords campaign or TV spot pays off, you know exactly what you can expect to spend for every new product sale that your team manages to execute. And you won't incur that cost until and unless an actual sale is made.

When thinking about how you'll calculate the return on the investment into an incentive program, it's also helpful to consider how you'll be accounting for the expense on your end-of-year profit and loss statement. For many of the clients that we work with, the types of incentive programs that we discuss in this book are categorized as marketing costs. This can be a good thing, depending on the structure of your organization.

Take a moment to consider your company's cost centers. Where are funds currently allocated? Where is there room for extra expenditures? In the case of your sales team, you're generally lumping commissions in with overall payroll expenses, the same as any other department in your organization. Perhaps you only have a fixed amount in the budget this year for payroll, and you want to use any extra funds that have been set aside to hire additional staff rather than grant raises or increase commission levels.

If you have extra funds available in your marketing budget, you can direct those funds to an incentive program for your sales team. This allows you to optimize your current sales levels without funneling additional money into payroll.

While other forms of marketing are important and shouldn't be neglected, none of them can really offer you guaranteed ROI. A good incentive program, though, can do precisely that. This fact alone is reason enough to allocate some of your organization's resources to the implementation of an incentivized rewards or recognition award program.

***

Now that we've discussed the ways that traditional advertising, digital marketing, and other forms of promotional revenue-generating techniques can fall short when it comes to ROI, and how that contrasts with a guaranteed return on investment using incentives, you're probably itching to implement an incentive program. But before you do, it's important to consider how this program will play out from the perspective of your employees and channel partners. For any incentive program to be effective, your team must understand it and identify with it. The better equipped they are to take advantage of a program, the better it'll work in the long run.

In the next chapter, we'll take a look at how to train and prepare your organization for a newly implemented incentive program. As we'll see, proper training can optimize the effectiveness of the program, the knowledge level of your employees, and the degree to which your employees identify with your company and brand as a whole.

Chapter 5

The Training Option

As the old saying goes: "Good help is hard to find." But when we say, "good help," what exactly are we talking about? As it turns out, there are a couple of things that make for an ideal employee or channel partner.

First, a good employee or channel partner understands your brand —and identifies with it. As a member of your organization, this person considers themselves to be a "part of the team" and they believe in your brand—in their brand. These kinds of employees are extremely valuable. They're proud to let people know just how great your brand really is. In addition to serving as walking, talking advertisements for your company, they'll bend over backwards to keep things on track with a project they're involved in.

Next, a good employee is educated, and that's not just holding a degree from college or some sort of vocational training that they obtained prior to starting work with you (although this kind of education can obviously be important, too). We mean that they've been educated in such a way as to maximize their utility for your company.

The specifics of this sort of education will look different for every organization, and sometimes even for every department within a larger organization. You might need to provide all of your employees with a base level of "brand identification education" in alignment with the first point above. In addition to that, though, specialized education that's particular to an individual department can go a long way. With the right training, an employee's productivity can go through the roof. Without that training, they may never reach their full potential.

Lastly, a good employee is motivated. They're excited to come to work because they know that their performance equals actual reward. Rather than simply clocking in, putting in their hours, being disengaged, clocking out, and heading home with a sigh of relief, a good employee operates at maximum capacity. And they're excited to be there, too, as each day at work presents a new opportunity.

The first two items—brand identification and education—can be achieved through proper training. The last item comes as a result of proper incentives. Incentives can be tied to training to maximize employee brand identification, education, and motivation simultaneously.

Drinking the Kool-Aid

In our experience working with larger organizations, there's typically one thing that comes up as both high on their priority list of things to achieve and also difficult to pull off: Getting their employees and channel partners to identify with their brand.

The larger a company is, the more difficult it becomes for an employee to self-identify with it. Think about it this way: If you're a sole proprietor with zero employees, identifying with your brand is easy. Literally, you're it. Not only are you the sole representative of your brand, you're also highly invested in its success. The same goes for a small business run as a partnership.

The next step away from this sort of sole proprietorship model for ease in brand identification is an early stage startup. An employee who comes aboard leading up to or immediately following the early funding stage probably identifies with the brand. There are a couple of reasons for this.

On the one hand, this engagement could very well be a chicken-and-egg scenario. Someone may be particularly interested in a startup's business model, idea, or product, and came on board for that reason. If so, they're identifying with the brand for personal reasons. And many early-stage startup employees tend to wear multiple hats and take ownership of more than one aspect of the company. They begin to see it as "theirs" as much as it is anyone else's. Perhaps most importantly, there's the reward factor. Early-stage startup employees often receive an equity incentive. And as we've seen throughout this book, incentives are the key to employee performance.

Once an organization gets to be quite large with a number of entry level employees, brand identification becomes diluted. The less invested an employee is in a company's success, the less likely they are to become a brand ambassador. And, similarly, an employee who stands to gain the least from a company's successes is also the least likely to identify with that brand.

So, how do you get your employees to drink the proverbial Kool-Aid? According to a study by Rico Piehler,[27] Chair of Innovative Brand Management at the University of Bremen, Germany, both effective internal brand management (IBM) and employee brand citizenship behavior (BCB) are to some degree a function of how well an employee understands a brand. This makes sense, of course. An employee who doesn't really understand what their company is all about will have a hard time identifying with it or articulating that identification to others.

What does this mean for your organization? Simply put, education is an important part of getting your employees to identify with your brand. The more your employees understand about your company, the more likely they are to identify with it. Also throw the proper incentives into the mix—that is, give your employees a real reason to care—and you'll be well on your way to a workforce of brand ambassadors.

Employee Education

When we talk about employee education, we're actually referring to a few different things simultaneously:

1. Education to indoctrinate your employees and turn them into effective brand ambassadors.

2. Education that improves your employee's overall knowledge and/or specific skills to increase productivity and performance.

3. Education to introduce your employees to an incentive program and ensure the maximum efficacy of that program.

Here, we'll be talking about item #2 on that list. But keep the others in mind, as they're all connected.

Just how important is this task-based knowledge and skill-specific education for employees? As it turns out, it may be a lot more valuable than you think. Let's look at some numbers.

First, it's worth pointing out just how little training most employees receive. At companies with under 100 employees, the average manager receives only 12 minutes of training[28] every 6 months. For companies with more than 100 employees, that number drops to a mere 6 minutes of training per 6 months. Meanwhile, employees clearly want more training than they receive. One study found that as many as 74% of workers[29] feel they could be performing better, but can't reach their full potential due to a lack of on-the-job training opportunities.

Granted, training employees takes time and resources. But a wealth of data points to just how effective proper training can be in terms of increasing revenue. The Association for Talent Development (ATD)[30] found that companies offering genuine training opportunities can offer 218% higher income per employee, while simultaneously achieving a 24% higher profit margin than companies that opt to spend less on training. Why such a large difference? It all comes down to better productivity. According to another study,[31] the National Center on the Educational Quality of the Workforce found that spending on employee education was significantly more effective in increasing productivity than other forms of investment. For example, a 10% spending increase in employee education resulted in an 8.6% increase in productivity, whereas the same spending increase on new (and seemingly more efficient) equipment only resulted in a corresponding 3.4% improvement in productivity.

The bottom line, then, is that proper training for your employees will increase your profit margins, your productivity, and even your employee retention rates. After all, employees who are earning more (per the first study) and who are able to perform their jobs skillfully and confidently are much less likely to leave for another position elsewhere. In fact, one Canadian study suggests that 40% of employees who fail to receive proper training end up leaving their job within the first year.

The question is, how do you get employees to actually participate in training? You may be able to force certain forms of training onto your employees as a condition of employment. This is how many employers approach it, in fact. If a new hire isn't willing to go through your organization's training program, then they won't be offered a position.

In terms of the carrot versus the stick, though, this can quickly devolve into a "stick scenario." Employees can feel bullied into completing a program they're not interested in. Particularly if you attempt to combine skills-based education with the kind of brand ambassador indoctrination discussed above, employees can quickly begin to tune out and even resent the experience. This can result in wasted educational resources as employees fail to get anything out of the educational process, and it can actually have the unintended consequence of *reducing* productivity and profitability, as employee performance dips following a boring, unengaging, and (in their minds) irrelevant series of educational sessions.

What you need is the proper carrot. Simply put, incentives are the key to effective employee training.

Incentives and Employee Training

When employees have a reason to participate in training, they'll be much more likely to retain and apply what they're learning. We all know how important attitude can be when it comes to taking full advantage of something, and nowhere is this truer than with employee education.

At the same time, though, incentive programs are only as effective as they are properly implemented. It's important, therefore, to ensure that your employees fully understand and can actively participate in whatever incentive program you choose to use as a means of increasing employee training buy-in. This is where incentives, employee education, and brand identification all come together. With the right approach, you can actually combine all three into one unified, seamless experience for your workforce.

Rather than attempting to indoctrinate your employees, train them in specific on-the-job skills, and bring them up to speed on how your new incentive program works...why not do all of these things at once?

Think of how effective this can be. As you're attempting to turn employees into brand ambassadors, they're constantly being reminded of the rewards-based incentives that await them. Meanwhile, you let them know about all of the other educational opportunities available to them when it comes to skills-specific training—all of which are also incentivized through further rewards. It's a win-win scenario for both you and your employees.

One of the best things about this sort of training combination is that you can deliver all (or most) of it online. While bringing employees into a classroom setting can present logistical challenges and added costs, offering an online training option to your employees can both reduce overhead expenses and increase the likelihood of compliance. Rather than forcing your employees to sit through a training session on a given day and time, they're given the freedom to go through training on their own schedule. More carrot, less stick.

If you're using an online rewards-based incentive platform or portal, you can provide this training directly through that same platform. This is a perfect environment for both brand indoctrination and incentive program education. Your employees will be using a branded interface, and they'll be working within the same platform that they'll later use to redeem their rewards. This gives them a chance to familiarize themselves with the platform, which means they'll be even more likely to use it in the future and participate actively in your organization's employee rewards program.

This is also the perfect opportunity to train your employees on your incentive program. While they're using the platform to complete some other form of education—whether it be introductory information to expose new employees to your brand, or a detailed and technical training for more senior employees—you'll have the chance to explain how your incentive program works. Your employees will be motivated to absorb this information, as they'll be eager to cash in on the rewards they've earned by completing their training. This kind of organized and thorough introduction to your incentive program will lead to better employee utilization of the platform and higher rates of program participation in the long run.

***

So far, we've touched on all of the most important foundational aspects of incentives. Now, it's time to dig into the nitty gritty of how incentive programs actually work. This is where the rubber meets the road.

In the next chapter, we'll discuss one of the most common forms of incentive programs that we offer for our clients' organizations, which is likely to be a program that your organization will want to offer, too: Incentive programs aimed at increasing sales via channel marketing.

Chapter 6

Salesperson Incentives

Have you ever worked in sales? Perhaps your organization employs a sizeable sales force, and you're interacting with your salespeople on a regular basis. Whether you've had firsthand experience working in sales or not, all it takes is a few minutes spent with a dedicated salesperson to realize that there's something unique about them.

People work different jobs for a whole host of reasons. Some people go into a particular line of work because it's emotionally rewarding. The job makes them feel useful and valuable, and they have the sense that they're contributing something important to the world each and every day they're at work. Other people are simply captivated by a particular topic or field and find themselves almost magnetically drawn to that job. And, of course, plenty of people end up in jobs that pay reasonably well, offer them a certain level of comfort and familiarity, and that they can count on as a reliable source of income for years to come.

Salespeople are different. Ask someone in sales why they do what they do, and you may indeed get a wide range of responses. Some people will tell you that they love meeting new people. They'll call themselves a "people person," and go on about how much satisfaction they get from working with customers. Other salespeople will talk up the product they sell or the company they work for, telling you all about how much they believe in the product or the organization.

To be fair, these reasons may indeed be true for some salespeople. But there's one thing that underlies just about every salesperson's desire to participate in this line of work, and some will cut straight to the chase and give it to you up-front. Here's the bottom line: When it comes to sales, it's all about the unlimited earnings potential.

Let's face it. There are all sorts of jobs out there and working in sales can be tough. If you've spent a day in a salesperson's shoes, you know exactly what we're talking about. Customers constantly shoot you down, telling you that they're not interested, or flat out ignoring you. It's exhausting work, and even the best salesperson will sometimes experience dry spells where income fluctuates considerably.

But in the end, all of this adversity is worth it for salespeople. Why? Not because it's what they always wanted to do ever since they were eight years old. It's because they can earn a serious amount of money based on their performance, and those earnings are virtually unlimited from year to year.

Keeping these motivations in mind is important when it comes to designing an incentive (or spiff) program for salespeople. We'll return to this point at the end of this chapter. For now, though, just remember: This chapter is all about incentives aimed at salespeople, and salespeople tend to respond to incentives that other employees may be less interested in or motivated by.

Sales Incentives for Channel Marketing

As we discussed earlier in this book, there are all sorts of options available to you when it comes to implementing an incentive program at your company. And all of these programs can drive increased revenue. Perhaps more than any other program format, though, sales incentives for channel marketing partners can produce huge dividends— and in a relatively short period of time. These are incentive programs aimed at independent sales reps who typically work for dealerships, distributors, and retail stores.

The reality is that effective channel marketing is difficult. When you're in control of every link in your sales chain (as is the case with direct B2C sales models, for instance), you can zero in on each and every aspect of the sales process. You control marketing, customer engagement, customer service—literally, everything. But when you're distributing products to third-party retailers, things are different because you don't get to call all the shots. In fact, you don't even get to manage your own sales force. Instead, you're at the mercy of salespeople who may or may not be interested in presenting your particular product to customers as their best or most viable option.

Channel marketing can also be quite challenging in very competitive industries and niches. Your products are side-by-side with several other, often very similar, options. A salesperson at a dealership or other independent retailer might have many reasons to recommend a competitor's product over yours, too. Maybe they've tried your competitor's product themselves, and they don't have any first-hand experience with yours. Or maybe—and this is the more likely scenario—there's some incentivized reason for them to sell that other product. Maybe their commission will be a little higher, and they're looking to rack up some extra income before the end of the quarter. Regardless of the specifics, it's easy to see how challenging it can be to ensure that your products get the attention and focus they deserve from salespeople at the end of a third-party sales channel.

That's where incentives come in. With a properly focused and implemented incentive program, you can give these salespeople a reason to push your product just a little bit harder than your competitors'. And if you do it right, you'll see impressive results in a short amount of time.

Remember: Don't let ego get in the way. It all comes back to influencing behavior. Your goal with this kind of channel marketing-focused salesperson incentive program isn't just to sell more of a particular product, it's to change a salesperson's behavior. And in order to do that, you need to consider the specific scenario you're aiming to tackle. Let's examine several common situations that crop up for large organizations dealing with third-party distribution and see how a well-implemented incentive program can address the needs of each of these scenarios.

Increasing Marketing Share: Competing Products at the Same Location

One of the most common problems for some of our clients has been trying to successfully compete with other products at the end of their sales chain. As we just discussed, there are only so many options available to you if you want to crank up your revenue in this sort of scenario. The people selling your products directly to consumers aren't actually your salespeople. They don't answer to you, and your company's products may only represent a handful amongst dozens (or hundreds, or thousands) of others they offer to their customers.

Fortunately, a good incentive program can dramatically increase market share in this situation. We're speaking from experience when we say that a year-over-year sales increase of 20% or more is a completely reasonable goal and achievable with a minimal amount of hassle.

A special note: Incentives for channel partners increase in importance if they can reasonably be considered a commodity. Ego aside, don't let your product's benefits fool you. Sure, you need to believe that your widget is significantly better than the competition's. But is it really that much better? Honestly? If the differences are negligible, and the channel partners would probably see it the same way, think of how much impact a sales incentive would have on improving market share. If they can sell two relatively comparable widgets, and your widget carries a $50 spiff, that will likely make the difference in which product they'll promote, steer customer towards, and ultimately sell.

Incentives to Balance Sales Across Products and Models

The automobile industry makes for a great object study in many of these scenarios. Why? In the United States, a car is something that almost everyone needs, and most can afford at one price point or another. At the same time, there's a huge range within the industry: Everything from cheap, efficient, economical vehicles up through expensive, gas guzzling luxury SUVs. If incentives can work in a variety of situations in a market as dynamic as the automobile industry, they can work anywhere.

Aside from increasing market share, incentives can also be used to balance a company's sales across various products and models. This is something we've helped our clients do, and which virtually any company can achieve with the right incentive program.

When oil and gas prices change significantly, automobile sales patterns often shift in parallel. Economy cars will sell faster when oil prices are high, while SUVs and other less-practical vehicles will sit on the lot. Customer preferences also can often change quickly. Perhaps the once-popular sedans are gathering dust at your local dealership while the compact SUVs are flying off the lot.

These kinds of market trends are inevitable, regardless of what industry you're talking about. Some companies try to constantly adjust production and marketing to roll with the punches, and there's no doubt that those are important levers to pull. But once you've got the foundation for an incentive program in place, you can simply adjust that program to meet your organization's changing needs.

When the economy cars are selling like crazy, you incentivize third-party salespeople to push SUVs. And when the SUVs start disappearing faster than you'd ever thought possible, you put powerful incentives in place to encourage salespeople to move as many compacts as possible. Whatever the specifics of your industry or niche might be, the bottom line is the same: If you have the framework of an incentive program ready to go, you simply incentivize salespeople to rebalance sales whenever necessary.

Selling off Old Stock

Channel marketing incentives aren't just helpful when it comes to balancing sales across products and models. You can also use them to help you sell off old stock. Need to empty out last year's inventory so that you can focus on marketing new products? Salesperson incentives are a great way to make that happen.

Some years ago, during the Great Recession, our firm connected with a company that was going out of business. They were sitting on a massive inventory of heavy trucks, and needed to liquidate that inventory as quickly as possible. We helped them put together a liquidation strategy, and their inventory virtually evaporated.

What did we do? In this particular case—because the situation was emergent, and the client needed to get rid of their inventory immediately—we recommended a combination of both salesperson incentives and heavy consumer-facing discounts. As a result, salespeople were incentivized to push the trucks on customers, while customers were heavily incentivized to purchase discounted vehicles.

Within a few short months, they'd managed to liquidate their entire inventory and could shut down without the massive losses associated with holding extra inventory.

Moving Surplus Inventory

Every organization does its best when it comes to sales projections and inventory planning. No company knowingly produces more of a product than they think they can sell. Still, it's impossible to predict the future perfectly. Try as you might, you'll inevitably end up in situations where you have excess inventory you need to move. And when that happens, salesperson incentives are a great way to achieve your goals in the shortest amount of time possible.

As in the case above, coupling consumer-facing product discounts with salesperson incentives is an effect way to move surplus inventory. You do have to be careful, since you don't want to go overboard with discounts, particularly with certain brands and products. As referenced earlier, excessive discounting can be damaging to your brand, so tread lightly.

Replacing Discounts with Incentives

In Chapter 4, we discussed some of the traditional ways that companies attempt to market and sell their products, and one method we looked at was the use of discounts and promotional offers. As we saw, discounts and promotions obviously have their place as part of an organization's overall sales strategy, but can sometimes be damaging to your brand reputation.

It's not just extreme situations like the grocery stores we discussed earlier that can be problematic when it comes to discounting, though. For some companies, discounts of virtually any kind can be damaging to brand image. If you're selling a premium product, attempting to use discounts to bring in new customers can tarnish the way your brand is perceived over time. With enough discounts put in place, your brand no longer appears to be premium to your customers. Next thing you know, you're competing with products and companies that were previously considered to be of a lower quality than what your company has to offer.

Fortunately, discounts and customer promotions aren't the only way to increase your sales. If you're in a position where you need to cut back on the amount of discounting you're doing—or where discounts don't fit well with your brand image in the first place—salesperson incentives can replace customer discounts, promotions, and rebates. In fact, a properly designed and implemented incentive program is likely to outstrip discount-based sales strategies when it comes to overall performance and return on investment.

Using Salesperson Incentives for the Right Products

There's no doubt that these kinds of salesperson incentives can be effective. In fact, we'd argue that they're often one of the best things you can do to increase your company's sales, particularly when it comes to specific products.

That last point, though, is worth noting. Salesperson incentives don't work for every single product out there. In fact, the modern consumer marketplace for the majority of products is such that these types of incentives *won't* work all that well. Let us explain.

In this day and age, consumers are savvier than they've ever been. Since the advent of the internet, it's become easier and easier to access information on the fly. Now, all a consumer has to do is pick up their phone if they want to determine which product best meets their needs (and best fits their budget).

You've likely noticed the explosion in consumer-facing "blog content" over the past few years. Now that placing in the top tier of search results becomes increasingly difficult, companies are racing to create useful, user-friendly web content that will help them achieve a top-ranking spot when a lead or customer searches for a particular product or keyword phrase. As a result, the internet is now replete with Top 10 lists, product guides, and side-by-side reviews and comparisons. If you want to know whether you should go with product A, B, or C—or if all three are a bad choice compared to product D—all it takes is a quick search to find out.

As a result, it's harder than ever for salespeople to influence consumer decision making, and that means you have to be careful about where you try salesperson incentives. If you pour time, energy, and resources into creating a salesperson incentive program for the wrong types of products, you simply won't see the type of return on investment you're looking for.

We recommend sticking to products that still require human interaction and a personal touch. Cars, jewelry, expensive watches, carpets and flooring, heavy machinery, kitchen cabinets, and other high-ticket items are still frequently purchased after a conversation between a salesperson and a consumer. For businesses, items like trucks, heavy equipment, parts, and other capital expenditures are often great targets. These sorts of expensive purchases often warrant expert input. Buyers actually *want* to have an interaction with a knowledgeable salesperson who can guide them toward the product that best fits their unique needs and desires. If your company manufactures these types of products, properly implemented incentives for salespeople can be highly effective.

The only exception to the above recommendation involves occasional product merchandising for lower-cost products. Whether it's a sporting goods retailer or a grocery store, the way products are displayed within a physical space can often have a dramatic impact on sales. That said, we've seen sales incentives be extremely effective at the retail level when they're targeted at managers, those people who have sway on the proper placement of your merchandise. Items as low as $1, yes one whole dollar, have seen positive impacts from a well-conceived program that helps to influence product merchandising.

Remember Your Target Market

We've talked here about how salesperson incentives can be an effective form of channel marketing and how these types of incentives can work for companies looking to increase market share, balance sales across products and models, sell off old stock, and move surplus inventory. We also discussed the potential of replacing discounts with incentives to achieve the same goals without tarnishing your brand's premium image.

But what's the most important thing of all when it comes to salesperson incentives for channel marketing? That's simple: You have to remember your target market. These incentives aren't aimed at your customer service reps, your product development team, or your customer base. They're targeted at salespeople, none of whom work directly for your company. Remember that salespeople are motivated by earning potential, and that your incentive program will have to play into this motivation if it's going to be effective. If this is your first time trying to implement such a program, consider connecting with a firm with specific experience in salesperson incentives for channel marketing. The wrong types of incentives won't produce the results that you want—but properly designed incentives can result in 20% (or more) year-over-year revenue increases.

***

At this point, you might be thinking, what about my employees? Are there incentive programs that will work well for people on my payroll? What if my company doesn't work with independent sales reps? In the next chapter, we'll take a look at how your organization can use incentives to influence employee behavior—and ultimately create the changes that you desire in your workforce.

Chapter 7

Incentives for Employee Behavior

In the last chapter, we looked at how incentive programs can be used to leverage an independent, third-party sales force. However, incentives can be just as powerful with your own employees. In fact, we've consistently seen that a properly implemented incentive program is one of the most effective ways to change employee behavior within an organization. In this chapter, we'll take a look at why you might want to use one or more rewards-based incentive programs within your organization, and how to make those programs work in the most effective ways possible.

Before we dive into all of the options available to you when it comes to employee incentive programs, let's take a moment to review some of the differences between these sorts of programs and the ones discussed in the last chapter.

When it comes to increasing revenue with third-party salesperson incentives, the scope of what you're trying to do is fairly narrow. In other words, your end goal is singular and straightforward: You want to increase sales of a particular product or range of products, and you need to incentivize a very specific type of personality (a salesperson) to make that happen. This means that measuring ROI is going to be relatively simple, as you'll essentially just be looking at sales numbers to assess your incentive program. It also means that the type of incentives you're using will almost always be cash-based (or points-to-cash) and directly connected to the act of closing a sale.

It's easy to get stuck in this revenue-based, cash incentives mindset. Sticking to this model across the board for incentives within your own organization, though, is a mistake.

Take a moment to survey your organization from the inside out. You likely have a wide range of internal departments, including accounting, finance, marketing, product development, purchasing and inventory, logistics, customer service, human resources, IT, and sales. Some of these departments could be quite large, and you might be dealing with a wide range of employees with different educational backgrounds and levels of experience.

Now, think about your company's goals. You surely want to increase revenue, but is incentivizing your salespeople to push your products harder the only way to increase revenue? Of course not. For one thing, potentially cutting costs could mean a higher profit margin, which can sometimes outstrip the potential profit increase associated with gains in revenue. Improving customer service can increase customer loyalty, which in turn can mean better customer lifetime value and higher sales numbers. There might be some less tangible but equally important things that you want to accomplish at your organization, too. Maybe you want to encourage better cooperation between coworkers. Or, perhaps, you want to incentivize your employees to live healthier lifestyles.

We'll discuss these and other goals in greater detail below. For now, just remember that incentives aren't just about increasing the number of zeros on a sales report. Incentives are about changing employee behavior, which can result in any number of changes within your organization—including, but not limited to, revenue growth.

The key is understanding that different employees in different departments, with different experiential and educational backgrounds will respond differently to various types of incentives. There are tried and true approaches to incentivizing behavior that we've seen work consistently well at our firm, but that doesn't mean that these are your only options. It's important to remember that every organization is unique, as is every department.

Those same differences hold true for the desires of the employees themselves. Some people have a strong preference for cash rewards, while others might prefer to receive travel incentives such as free hotel stays. Still others might prefer to see their monthly health insurance premium decreasing, thus giving them the opportunity to reallocate those funds in their monthly budget. And of course, don't forget extra PTO (paid time off), which technically costs nothing but can be highly valued by family-oriented workers.

The important thing is to remember that, above all else, you must know your company. Whether it's through surveys, vast experience or common sense, you know the people in your organization's various departments. Keep this in mind throughout the chapter and think about how these individuals' intrinsic motivations can be leveraged most effectively to influence their behavior.

Incentivizing Employee Behavior

As mentioned above, there are a number of different types of behavioral changes that you might want to incentivize in your employees. These changes will be directly connected to your company's current goals. Your company might want to achieve one of the following goals:

- Improved employee health markers
- Changes to the working environment
- Greater employee engagement in charitable work
- Better teamwork in teams
- Higher customer service ratings and greater customer satisfaction

...and the list goes on.

Let's take a look at a few of these potential goals and see how you might incentivize employee behavioral changes in order to achieve them.

Employee Health and Health Care Costs

Year after year, health care costs continue to rise. Employers offering health insurance, as many organizations are now mandated to do, pay a large portion of these premiums. On average, employers cover about 80% of individual plan and 70% of family plan premium costs, respectively.

Even though it's now illegal for insurance companies to discriminate based on an individual's health history and preexisting conditions, there's no doubt that the overall health of a group does indeed continue to affect group health insurance purchasing options and prices. According to the American Academy of Actuaries,[32] "premiums will be higher on average whenever a "risk pool disproportionately attracts those with higher expected claims." At the same time, the reverse is also true: Whenever a "risk pool disproportionately avoids those with higher expected claims," or if the risk pool is able to "offset the costs of those with higher claims by enrolling a large share of lower-cost individuals," overall premium prices for the entire group's coverage will be lower.

Both of these points are particularly salient when you consider how health care costs and spending are often spread across individuals. According to a study from the National Business Group on Health,[33] the average high-cost claimant logged $122,382 in annual claims, roughly 30x the claims cost of the average individual. In other words, this means that around 1% of those covered under a group insurance policy are responsible on average for roughly 31% of the health care costs associated with that group. And of these high-cost claims, more than half are associated with longstanding, chronic conditions—not acute conditions related to accidents or other unforeseeable circumstances.

So, what does all of this mean for employers? It's simple: The healthier your employees are, the lower the risk to insurance companies and the less you'll pay for your portion of your employees' premiums. When your employees are engaging in healthy activities and behaviors, they're reducing the occurrence of chronic conditions and cutting back on their use of prescription medications and trips to the doctor. The less your employees are using their benefits, the lower your group's premium costs should be from year to year. Even if rates don't go down, as employees reduce the reliance on health insurance, they'll be spending less and less on deductibles, office visits, and other out-of-pocket expenses. This frees up money for other expenses, and can potentially add to increased well-being.

Simply asking your employees to engage in healthy behaviors isn't going to cut it though. As we've seen, humans alter their behavior in response to incentives, and dominant thinking is short-term. You've got to give your employees a tangible reason to make changes. Old habits are hard to break, particularly those surrounding diet and physical activity.

Keep in mind that your incentive spending doesn't have to be massive on a per-employee basis. A recent RAND Corporation study[34] found that 84% of employees will participate in a wellness incentive program that costs employers as little as $5 a week, or about $250 a year.

The key is making sure you tailor incentives to the individual wants, needs, and health conditions of your employees, because one size doesn't fit all. Consider incentivizing employees with chronic conditions to keep up with annual wellness visits. For employees with diabetes who would benefit from weight loss, you might incentivize them to take a certain number of steps each day. (And with smart watches, tracking these activities into a custom portal is easier than ever.) Next thing you know, they're going for a walk on their lunch break. For employees experiencing pregnancy, you could incentivize adherence to a good prenatal health strategy.

Keep in mind that these kinds of health and wellness incentives don't just reduce your annual health insurance expenditures. They can produce a synergistic effect across your entire organization. When most of your employees are eating better and moving more, fewer employees call in sick. Healthier employees can even contribute indirectly to revenue growth, as healthier workers are likely to be more productive over the course of a day, week, month, or year.

Employee health is important and neglecting it can cost you. With the right incentive programs—that is, by using the right carrot—you can slowly shift employee behavior in the right direction.

Charitable Work

The Tampa Bay Lightning hockey team values charitable work so much that giving has become a vital aspect of each home game. During the second TV timeout, the team unveils its latest "Community Hero," local leaders who've given their time, money, or resources to bettering the Tampa Bay community. Complete with a video montage on the scoreboard, the team issues a $50,000 grant to that hero's specified charity. With tens of millions of dollars donated over several years, the fans preemptively rise to their feet in a standing ovation before the check is even presented. Not every company has the financial resources, or fan base, of the Tampa Bay Lightning. But that doesn't mean that increasing charitable giving shouldn't be a goal.

Employee giving and charity work has become an increasingly common part of corporate work culture, with a number of purported benefits associated with it. For one thing, it gives your employees a chance to diversify their focus and "get away from work" for a brief period—a kind of working vacation. For another, certain types of employee giving can foster team-building and worker cooperation. And, of course, allowing your employees to select their own charity gives them the satisfaction of investing their time and energy in something they genuinely care about. They'll then link this opportunity to your company, increasing their overall affinity for your organization.

As with the health and wellness example above, the effects of properly implemented employee giving programs can be significant and synergistic. First though, you have to actually get employees to engage in them.

There's plenty of data available that points to the various ancillary benefits of employee charity work. Some of it is particularly surprising, too. A recent study from the University of Southampton[35] suggests that linking a charitable gift to work performance can boost productivity by as much as 13%. And when employees can choose their contribution level and recipient, that number climbs to a staggering 26%.

As with any behavioral change, though, getting your employees to take the first step can be difficult. If you've ever taken up exercising after a long stint of inactivity, you know exactly what we're talking about. A couple of weeks into a new routine, you start to feel great. It becomes its own reward, and no one needs to convince you to keep doing it. But those first few sessions are tough, and a big part of you is ready to throw in the towel, skip the workout, and go grab a burger and beer instead. Once your employees start participating in some form of charitable giving, they'll likely want to continue after experiencing its positive effects. But first, you have to give them a nudge.

Incentives for employee giving can take a variety of forms. One option involves simply matching employee gifts dollar for dollar, or at some other ratio up to a limited total. An increasingly popular incentive is the so-called "paid release day," where employees are allotted a certain number of paid days per year to go work with a local charitable organization. While employees may not be eager to spend their Saturday pitching in with a local charity, giving them the option of working a four-day week and volunteering on Friday can be significantly more appealing.

In the same way, company-wide charity workdays can be a great way to give employees a break from the office, improve morale, and build a greater sense of cooperation. Your employees get to spend a day outside of their standard 9-to-5 environment doing something that makes them feel good—that is, giving back to the community—while interacting with their fellow workers in a new setting. This can foster new relationships and connections between employees. Rather than making the charity day a paid workday, though, you can incentivize participation in this type of an event on a non-workday with a reloadable debit card or other form of cash reward.

Customer Service

If you take the long view when it comes to company growth and increased revenue, customer service may be the single most important thing to focus on improving. The numbers tell the story quite clearly here. According to the Harvard Business Review,[36] finding and acquiring new customers can be anywhere from 5 to 25 times more expensive than retaining the customers you already have, depending on what industry you're in. Just as astoundingly, increasing customer retention by as little as 5% can increase total profits—not revenue, but profits—by up to 95%. Yes, that's right: retaining an extra 5% of customers can in some cases actually *double profits* for your organization.

This makes sense when you think about it. Consider all of the expenses associated with finding new customers. Marketing costs can run into the many millions of dollars for larger ad campaigns and employing a sizeable sales force can get expensive quick. Meanwhile, retaining customers is largely a matter of providing good customer service. And while there have to be certain systems in place for quality customer service to be possible, much of what the average customer perceives to be outstanding or abysmal service ultimately comes down to one thing: the way your employees treat your customers.

When a customer calls in with an issue, their experience can go one of two ways. They could connect with an employee who's genuinely apologetic, knowledgeable, and helpful, and who solves their problem for them quickly and efficiently—and maybe even goes the extra mile to offer them something small to compensate them for their trouble. Or they might encounter an employee who's disinterested, irritable, lacking in understanding, and completely unhelpful.

In the former scenario, the customer's brand affinity goes through the roof. They go from being a customer with a complaint to a lifetime advocate for your brand. In the latter, they never buy from you again—and may take the time to post a negative review or two online. And, whenever your company comes up in conversation, they'll be sure to let everyone know just how awful you are.

It's easy to see just how essential good customer service really is for your organization. And that's why incentivizing improvements in customer satisfaction can be so effective for overall growth.

Customer service-based incentive programs are becoming increasingly common, and we've seen them work time and again. These programs don't have to be complicated, either. Introducing one can be as simple as offering your customer service employees prepaid debit cards if they're able to increase their customer satisfaction scores by a certain percentage, or to a certain baseline number. This kind of simple, inexpensive, easy-to-implement incentive program can send customer retention through the roof. And considering the statistics, modest spending on such an incentive program is well worth even a small increase in customer retention.

Teamwork

One important employee characteristic that we haven't touched on yet is one that you'll encounter in every successful organization or department. We're talking about teamwork. It's easy to roll your eyes and discount the idea of improving employee comradery. Many of us have been through entire workshops filled with ineffective, almost painfully patronizing "team building exercises." But developing teamwork effectively is one of the most important things you can do for your company, and it's something that you can't afford to overlook. The question is how to do it correctly, without making your employees feel like they're trapped in a bad situation comedy.

Just like with other employee behaviors, an improvement in both teamwork and overall comradery and mutual recognition between employees can be achieved with the proper incentives. One of the great things about focusing on a behavior like teamwork is just how synergistic it can be. When your employees start working together and mutually acknowledging one another's contributions to both individual projects and the company as a whole, everything else at your organization will begin to function optimally. Deadlines will be met more frequently. The office atmosphere will be more enjoyable. Customer satisfaction will increase. Sales numbers will improve. And though it may be difficult to measure using a quarterly report, people will be happier.

Some time ago, our firm was contracted by a large *Fortune* 500 client to help improve teamwork and boost morale. Rather than sending their employees off to workshops or sending out mandatory literature on working as a team, they opted to go the incentive route.

Our client ordered a large number of $25 prepaid branded debit cards and sent them out to department heads all across the country. These department heads then informed the employees they supervised that a new program was being put into place. The way it worked was simple. If an employee noticed that a coworker was acting in a way that exemplified top teamwork, they could request a prepaid debit card for that employee and then hand it over to them. Employees would thus be directly rewarded for engaging in behavior that was conducive to team building.

The program was a huge hit. Before long, employees were going out of their way to help their colleagues and be better team players. Our client was so satisfied with the morale boost and the measurable improvements involved that they opted to order more debit cards. It was a win-win for everyone: Employees got extra spending money, the atmosphere at work was dramatically improved, and our client achieved their goal of improved teamwork and better cooperation between employees.

The best part about using incentives to modify behaviors like teamwork and cooperation is that employees don't feel manipulated or talked down to. Sending an employee to an all-day workshop where they're told that they need to behave differently can actually have the opposite effect of what's desired. This is a classic carrot vs. stick example. If you're presented with a choice between a stick and a carrot to achieve your end goal, there's no contest: The carrot always wins.

***

In this chapter, we identified some of the different behaviors and outcomes that you can incentivize. These kinds of behavioral incentives become particularly powerful when they're implemented together. Don't feel like you have to choose a single behavior to incentivize. Depending on the size of your organization and the complexity of the task at hand, it may be a good idea to start with a single program and outcome before expanding. Eventually, though, it's completely possible to run multiple incentive programs simultaneously across different departments, branches, and locations. As the saying goes, the sky's the limit.

So far, we've looked at incentives that you can use for both your own employees and independent sales reps. These kinds of incentives are inward-looking: They're directed at your supply chain, rather than at the people who are actually purchasing your products. In the next chapter, we'll take a look at an equally important and highly effective angle, incentives for customers.

Chapter 8

Incentives for Customers: Rebate Programs

Up until now, we've focused almost exclusively on the value and efficacy of incentive programs for the supply side of your business. While incentives will likely be different based on whether they're used for your own employees or independent sales reps, these kinds of supply chain incentives share a number of things in common. Any employee or sales rep program that you put into place will be targeted at the people in charge of producing, marketing, and selling your product, and/or those who interact with your customers.

Now we'll shift our focus to an alternative approach to incentives that's both highly effective and often underused by organizations of all sizes: Customer rebate programs.

Customer Rebates as Incentives

Customer rebates are without a doubt one of the oldest forms of incentive marketing. They've been around forever, and it's easy to overlook them as a viable option. They aren't quite as hyped as some newer approaches to marketing and customer retention, and the word "rebate" isn't exactly a sexy marketing term. They also may not seem like an incentive at first, as we tend to lump them together with coupons and discounts (which, incidentally, are forms of incentives nonetheless). Rebates are indeed incentives, though, and they can be incredibly effective at increasing sales and improving customer satisfaction when used correctly.

Setting up and initiating rebate programs is easier today than ever. Everything used to be manual and required significant time and costs. Customers would have to mail in vouchers, which employees would then have to receive, sort, verify, and pay out individually. This involved paying for postage both ways, along with the added cost of cutting a check and compensating your employees for their time.

Thanks to the wonders of the internet, though, paper rebates are no longer necessary. Now customers can simply log onto a website or download a mobile app in order to redeem a rebate. While this may reduce breakage rates somewhat (something we'll discuss in greater detail below), it improves customer satisfaction considerably. Filling out a paper form and mailing it in requires a significant amount of time and energy, whereas a form on a mobile app can be filled out and submitted in less than a minute.

Preserving Brand Equity

One of the biggest advantages of customer rebates is their ability to preserve brand equity.

Previously, we juxtaposed incentive programs with other approaches to increasing revenue, including the use of sales and discounts. As we mentioned, sales and discounts are an essential component in any business's marketing strategy, and they usually have their place in an effective and comprehensive sales model.

That said, though, we also pointed out that sales and discounts can cause major problems in the long run if over-used. This is especially true for premium brands that have sculpted a quality-before-price image for themselves—in other words, brands that have convinced their customers that it's worth spending a little more in order to obtain a quality or trendy product manufactured by XYZ Corp.

But excessive discounts can quickly tarnish the image of a premium brand, with all of the so-called brand equity you've built disappearing in a hurry. Before long, your brand is no longer premium. Customers come to expect that your products will be at the same price point as less-premium, lower-quality alternatives. To put it simply: discounting can quickly become a race to the bottom.

Rebates present a very different picture to your customers since they're perceived differently from a sale or discounted item because the original price hasn't changed. When a customer encounters a rebate, the image of your brand isn't tarnished in their mind. Brand equity is preserved, as you're offering them an opportunity to receive an exclusive reward—for example, a branded prepaid debit card—in exchange for purchasing one of your products.

This means that you can effectively offer a dollar-based rebate that equals a 20% discount, for example, rather than discounting an item by 20%. You never have to lower your premium prices, which means the customer never actually sees a lower price associated with an item: They see the original price, accompanied by a rebate. The end result is the same in that they save 20%, but the difference for your brand image can be considerable.

Better Breakage for Higher Profits

When it comes to rebate programs, we often talk about something called breakage. In layperson's terms, this refers to the number of customers who actually fulfill a rebate versus those who purchase the item with the intention of getting the rebate but fail to follow through. If 3 out of every 10 customers fails to actually claim their rebate, you would have a breakage of 30% for that product.

As we mentioned above, the easier it is for customers to claim their rebate, the lower your breakage rate can be. Obviously, breakage isn't a factor at all when it comes to sales and discounts, as every customer simply receives the discount up front. This is significant, as it means that the higher your breakage is, the higher percentage of rebate you're able to offer your customers without any further actual reduction in your revenue.

Think of it this way. Imagine that you were to offer a 30%-off sale for a product that's normally $100. Dropping the price of the product from $100 to $70 could have a negative impact on brand equity, as that's a major visual difference that consumers could quickly become accustomed to (leaving them averse to the $100 price tag when it comes back after the sale is over). If you sell 10 of these items, you're looking at $700 in sales.

Meanwhile, consider what would happen if you offered a whopping 40% rebate on the same item—but with a breakage rate of 50%. If you sell 10 of these items for $100, that's $1,000 in sales. Five of your customers then redeem their rebate, worth $40 each. That's $200 in rebates, leaving you with $800 in sales. You've therefore effectively increased total revenue by more than 14% ($800 as opposed to $700), while offering each and every one of your customers a higher discount (40% rather than 30%). It's a win-win for you, your brand, and your customers.

Believe it or not, a breakage rate of 50% isn't unheard of. In his book *Why Popcorn Costs So Much At the Movies: And Other Pricing Puzzles,* Richard B. McKenzie cites a study reporting that breakage rates can average 40% in certain industries. The key is striking the right balance in the redemption process: Make it easy enough so that customers don't become frustrated, but not so easy that you cut into your breakage rate any more than you have to.

Online Rebate Portals and Mobile Apps

While paper rebates are still an option—and may have their merits in certain situations—digital rebates have quickly become the norm across most industries. Fortunately, setting up an online or mobile-based rebate portal doesn't have to be complicated or expensive. Plus, there's the added advantage of automation once everything is in place. No need for employees to manually verify each rebate and send out a physical check in the mail: Much of it can be accomplished automatically.

We frequently work with clients who want to set up a rebate program for the first time or improve the efficiency of an existing program. Without exception, we opt to set up a custom rebate portal for our clients. These custom websites will typically (but not always) include supporting documentation collection (as needed), automatic email confirmation upon receipt of a customer's rebate request, email and/or phone-based customer service, and automatic rebate fulfillment.

Increasing Brand Affinity

One of the best things about rebates is they can further increase brand affinity in your customers. In the rebate vs. discount example above, we were only measuring the value of a rebate as opposed to a discount in terms of immediate revenue. In the long run, the discount runs the risk of damaging your brand. Meanwhile, the rebate can actually increase your customers' sense of loyalty toward your brand.

Much of this increased affinity is subconscious. Imagine what happens if you pay out a rebate in the form of a prepaid, branded debit card rather than a check. When your customer receives a check with their rebate, they likely deposit it and never think about it again. They feel a brief sense of affinity for your brand when the money hits their account, after which the funds are commingled with their existing account balance. Any memory of your brand falls by the wayside.

Alternatively, think about the impact that a prepaid branded debit card can have on a customer. They may carry that card in their wallet for months and swipe it for a variety of purchases. Each time they go to use the card, they'll see your company's logo. Subconsciously, they'll associate the satisfaction of the purchase with your brand. Over time, this can result in a significant increase in brand affinity.

The same holds for using a mobile app for claiming a rebate. Imagine that your brand has a mobile app which could be leveraged to better retain and market to customers, but which your customers simply aren't downloading. Offering a rebate that can only be claimed through your company's app gives your customers a reason to download it. This means more opportunities to effectively market to these customers with push notifications, not to mention the added bonus of your logo on their home screen every time they pull out their phone. Realistically though, these types of mobile apps are primarily desirable for businesses with regular customer interaction, such as restaurants, grocery stores or gas stations.

Brand affinity is incredibly valuable and retaining customers is infinitely more cost-effective than trying to find new ones. By increasing brand affinity, you'll increase both customer lifetime value and customer retention rates. Over time, this can lead to dramatic increases in revenue and general improvements across your organization.

***

Effectively leveraging rebates to improve sales, brand affinity, and overall customer loyalty is a good place to start when it comes to incentivizing customer behavior. But there's even more you can do.

In the next chapter, we'll take a look at customer loyalty programs. With the proper loyalty program in place, you'll be able to push brand affinity, customer lifetime value, and overall revenue to new levels.

Chapter 9

Customer Loyalty Programs

Competition is everywhere and it doesn't matter what industry you're in either. No matter how niche you think your business might be, any profitable niche will eventually attract competitors. Particularly in the era of the startup, no company is invincible when it comes to potential competitors.

Once you lose sight of this reality, you run the risk of being left behind. Regardless of what industry you're operating in, staying afloat in the modern world of business means ensuring that you're doing two things. First, you have to stand out from the crowd. And second, you've got to understand and reward your customers.

Customer loyalty programs are the perfect way to achieve both of these goals simultaneously. In this chapter, we'll look at why customer loyalty programs matter, how they work, and what you can do to ensure that your organization's customer loyalty program is optimized for success.

Stay On Their Minds

If you want to keep customers around, you have to work hard to stay top-of-mind. With people receiving upwards of 200 emails a day and scrolling endlessly through an advertising-laden social media stream, keeping your customers aware of your brand is more challenging than ever. That's why you need an effective customer loyalty program: It's one of the best ways to ensure that your customers don't forget about you. You're giving them a monetary incentive in the form of some sort of reward to keep coming back to your business, rather than choosing another alternative.

Let's be honest here, rewards may not be particularly important to you as an individual consumer. You may not make many purchasing decisions based on the potential to earn an incremental amount of rewards with a particular company. And the same may be true for a significant portion of your customers. Some of them simply won't care whether you offer rewards or not.

But for other customers, loyalty programs are everything. They make a point of choosing to patronize businesses that take the extra step to reward them for their loyalty. If your competitors offer rewards and you don't, you'll quickly lose these particular customers.

Plus, as we'll see below, rewards aren't just about satisfying a certain segment of your customers. With the right rewards program, you'll be able to amass huge amounts of customer-purchase data, which is invaluable in targeting your marketing efforts, resulting in more effective (and more affordable) marketing over the long haul.

The Technical Side of Customer Loyalty Programs

So far, we've looked at incentive programs targeted at independent sales reps, in-house employees, and also discussed customer rebates. All these incentives can be set up with a fairly simple, standalone web portal. There's no need to integrate these incentives with existing company systems, apart from collecting data for accounting purposes. In a sense, these types of incentives are independent of other technologies that your company might be leveraging.

With a customer loyalty program, though, things tend to get a bit more complicated. More often than not, you're rewarding customers based on purchases that they're making. As a result, you'll need to tie your loyalty program into your organization's existing point-of-sale (POS) system, which could involve hundreds or even thousands of store locations nationwide (assuming you have a brick and mortar element). This kind of integration can be complicated. Generally speaking, implementing this type of incentive program will mean extensive IT integration with your POS, along with maintaining sizeable backend databases.

This isn't necessarily a bad thing. As we already mentioned, part of what you're looking to do with a customer loyalty program is collect as much data as possible. The better your POS-to-database integration, the more data you'll

133

have access to down the road. The takeaway here is that the type of company you'll likely need to work with for this sort of customer loyalty program will differ somewhat from the types of companies offering other incentive programs. In other words, don't be surprised if a provider that typically sets up rebate programs, employee rewards, and so on isn't capable of offering these types of POS integrations to you.

Keeping Things Simple

All of that said, it's completely possible to avoid some of the technical complications associated with a typical customer loyalty program. There's no need to assume that a loyalty program isn't doable just because you need to keep costs down or simplify the initial setup process.

Rather than going the POS-and-database route, you can simply set up a customer loyalty program that works like a rebate. With this type of loyalty program, customers use an app to scan the barcode on an item they've purchased or enter the barcode number manually via an online portal. Their activity is tracked through an account, and they later receive rewards based on the purchases that they've manually entered into their purchase history.

Fresh Step Cat Litter's Paw Points program[37] functions much in this way. As the name implies, it's a points-based program where customers can rack up points by logging purchases into the Paw Points app. These points can later be redeemed for things like cat toys, cat condos, and so on.

Fresh Step also knows their customers. They're aware that many of their customers care about animal rescue and want to support their local animal shelter. So, rather than cashing in their points for themselves, customers have the option of donating their points to a local shelter so they can receive much-needed toys, cat litter, beds, and more.

The success of Fresh Step's program is evidence that any company—large or small—can opt to go the simpler, rebate-based route rather than tracking customer activity through a POS system. Your budget and your company's needs and goals can determine which direction you choose to go.

What a Customer Loyalty Program Can Do

Before we go into detail about what you can do to increase the efficacy of your customer loyalty program, let's take a look at what a successful customer loyalty program can do.

In 2012, Walgreens launched its Balance Rewards program.[38] At the time, Walgreens was struggling, losing market share to CVS and RiteAid, with sales that had flattened out and fallen off slightly over the past few years. CVS had an extensive customer-loyalty program already in place, and Walgreens had to start from scratch. They realized that a good loyalty program was key to staying competitive. So, as part of a nationally coordinated campaign, they launched the Balance Rewards program[39] at more than 7,900 stores nationwide in September of 2012. Since then, Walgreens has grown the rewards program to more than 150 million registered members, including 85 million active rewards members.

As a result, Walgreens now has access to a huge customer database with massive amounts of customer data. They've used this data to personalize their marketing. One example is the way they're targeting their marketing efforts based on a customer's "propensity to buy" score. The top one third with the highest propensity to buy are enrolled in a "Thank You" program, receiving special rewards offers via email and direct mail, along with a product sample intended to compel them to purchase. The middle third of customers receive various placement ads and coupons. Finally, the bottom third—the ones with the lowest propensity to buy—are exposed to various digital display and paid search ads. When they click on these ads, they're directed to a page on the Walgreens website that educates them about the brand itself. According to Walgreens' Director of Supply Marketing, Lisa Zhao, the customers exposed to these campaigns develop much higher Net Promoter Scores than customers who have no exposure to them.

The Walgreens story demonstrates how essential it is to take the long view with customer loyalty, along with the value of customer data in personalized marketing. Walgreens saw a gross sales increase of 65% over the first five years of the Balance Rewards program. And most of those gains didn't start happening until the loyalty program had been in effect for a couple of years. Walgreens' success is evidence of just how effective a customer loyalty program can be when executed properly.

Tips for an Effective Customer Loyalty Program

If you're going to go all-in with a new loyalty program, you'll need to do everything you can to make it successful.

Obviously, the last thing you want is to spend a considerable amount of resources (time, money, personnel) on a program that never gets off the ground or offers no measurable returns. So, let's take a look at five tips for making your loyalty program as effective as possible.

Tip #1: Consistency and Commitment

This might seem obvious at first glance. But you'd be amazed by how often this basic necessity is overlooked by companies large and small.

Before you dive in, take a moment to acknowledge that a full-fledged customer loyalty program is a long-term commitment. If you decide to pull out after only a few months, it could actually result in customer loss. People tend to react negatively to the cancellation of a loyalty program. Put yourself in one of your customer's shoes here: You spend hundreds (perhaps thousands) of dollars with a company, rack up a ton of rewards points, and then go to cash them in... only to find out that the program was discontinued last month. You can bet that you've not only lost that customer—you've created a fervent detractor.

Then consider the opposite scenario. A well-designed customer loyalty program backed by your organization's full commitment can boost customer confidence in your company,[40] which is one of the single most important factors when it comes to increasing customer lifetime value.

There's one other element of consistency and commitment that we should mention, too. It has less to do with following through with your program, and more to do with branding consistency. Make sure you offer branding consistency throughout your web portal, app, promotional emails, graphic design, and so on. You want to create a brand image for your loyalty program that customers can instantly recognize no matter the interaction point.

Tip #2: Keep It Simple

We'll be blunt here: Your customers don't want to deal with a complex, difficult-to-understand rewards program. At best, they'll ignore it. At worst, it will actively turn them off and send them packing to one of your competitors.

Remember that your customers are busy, and you're not the only company they patronize. They won't be able to keep track of complicated tier systems, personalization options, impossible password combinations, and so on. The simpler things are, the higher the chances of an individual customer participating. And more participation means a more successful and effective program.

To keep things simple, you'll want to minimize program options, ensure that your program is easy to join, and clearly communicate both point accumulation and spending rules to your customers. Make sure that it's easy to quickly and fully understand how your program works. If customers are left scratching their heads, they're unlikely to actually take part in your program.

Tip #3: Exclusivity

In some cases, the way that you present your program is just as important as what you're actually offering. To some degree, it's actually *more* important.

Don't get us wrong: Pointless rewards that add up to nothing are not going to increase customer retention. But presentation is an essential element in the total package. You want to tap into your customers' fear of missing out (FOMO), and one effective way to do that is to make your program feel as exclusive as possible. They've joined a special club, and they're going to get access to rewards that other people are missing out on.

Membership cards are one way to create exclusivity. A thoroughly branded web portal can accomplish the same thing. And, of course, a branded, custom debit card is the ultimate in exclusivity. We'll talk more about these in the next chapter.

Tip #4: The Psychology of the 'Head Start'

Have you ever signed up for a loyalty program that gives you a little sign up bonus? This makes joining feel more like it's worth the trouble and encourages you to start spending right away to add to your existing points.

This isn't just an isolated phenomenon, or something that simply "sounds" effective. A recent study[41] from researchers at USC and the Wharton School demonstrates that consumers are more likely to participate in such a program if they perceive themselves as having a head start.

In the study, participants were divided into two groups. One group was handed a loyalty punch card with a specific number of holes in it, and with some of the holes already punched out. The other group received the same punch card with an identical number of holes, but with none of them punched out. The not-so-surprising results? Subjects in the first group were statistically much more likely to participate in the program than those in the second group.

Giving your customers a sign-up bonus is also a great way to incentivize enrollment in your program when you launch it. Make the sign-up bonus temporary. In other words, customers have to sign up today, or this week, or no later than a specified date to receive the bonus. This will tap into their fear of missing out and can significantly improve your initial enrollment numbers.

Tip #5: The Right Partner(s)

Lastly—and perhaps most importantly of all—you must ensure that you're working with the right partner(s) when it comes to launching a customer loyalty program.

As we mentioned above, certain programs will require experienced partners prepared to do relatively complicated database and backend work to tie the program into your existing POS system. In other cases, you may be better off working with a company whose focus and expertise is less technical and more centered on branding, customer psychology, and so on.

The important thing is to be clear about what your needs are from the beginning and find a partner that can meet your needs, whatever they may be. Check their references before signing a contract and be certain that they've produced solid results for other organizations. Use the information you learn in this chapter (and throughout this book) to ask specific and pointed questions about how they plan to implement the new program. If they seem uncertain or lacking in experience, go elsewhere.

***

Now that you know how effective customer loyalty programs can be and have a good sense of what makes for a successful program, it's time to put one into action. Once you start to see results, you'll be glad that you did.

In the next several chapters, we'll shift gears to the nuts and bolts of how to run a program. Much of the information to come applies to a variety of incentive programs, whether they're targeted at third-party sales reps, your own employees, or your customers. To start, we'll look at how to use branded reloadable, prepaid, and virtual debit cards as your reward delivery system.

Chapter 10

Incentive Type: Branded Reloadable, Prepaid, and Virtual Debit Cards

There are multiple options available to you when it comes to implementing an incentive program. In terms of how rewards are actually delivered, you have lots of options, too. You might choose to simply reward a participant with a check, or by transferring funds into their account via ACH/direct deposit.

But as we've seen, these methods of reward delivery are less than ideal. Debit cards are often a far superior option if you want to create maximum loyalty and brand affinity while keeping things simple for both the issuer (your organization) and the recipient (an employee, third-party sales rep, or customer).

Let's take a closer look at the available options when it comes to using a debit card as your rewards-delivery mechanism, including reloadable branded debit cards, branded prepaid debit cards, and virtual debit cards. In the next chapter, we'll look at points-based systems that can be used to redeem merchandise and other rewards through an online platform.

A Note on the Word 'Debit'

Before we go any further, though, it's worth taking a moment to address the use of the phrase "debit card" here, and particularly the word "debit" itself.

Here in the United States, over 90% of Americans have a checking account[42] of some kind and, generally speaking, most people are pretty familiar with the idea of a debit card. They have a bank account that holds a certain amount of funds and, when they swipe their debit card somewhere, the account is "debited" for the same amount as the purchase. The bank then transfers the funds to the seller after a certain period of time. To use their debit card and thus have direct access to debiting their account, the card user must often enter a PIN code associated with their account for verification purposes.

Technically speaking, none of the card types we discuss in this chapter are actually proper "debit" cards, even though they have the word "debit" printed on them above the Visa or MasterCard logo. Instead, they fall under the "prepaid card" category. There are a couple of significant differences[43] between these cards and those issued by banks along with checking accounts (which are proper debit cards).

Firstly, debit cards are tied to a specific "demand deposit account" (i.e. a checking account) and thus fall under Regulation E, a Federal Reserve regulation covering certain electronic funds transfers. Meanwhile, prepaid cards are connected to a so-called omnibus account. The omnibus account owner is usually the organization which issues the card itself.

Secondly, prepaid cards must be signed in order to be used. Proper debit cards can sometimes be used without entering a PIN, but in this case, they're not actually processed as debit cards. In order to process a card as a debit card, the card's associated PIN must be entered.

The naming confusion came after an antitrust lawsuit was filed against both Visa and MasterCard regarding the rates (specifically the differences in rates) charged to retailers for running different types of cards, along with the types of cards they would accept. There's generally a cost disparity when it comes to processing a credit card transaction, which requires a signature, and a debit card transaction, which requires a PIN code. While prepaid cards do require a signature like a credit card, they're still typically referred to as debit cards.

In other words, the term "debit card" is a bit of a misnomer for the various prepaid card types discussed here, but it's still the industry standard term—and it even appears written on the cards themselves.

A special note: The cards discussed in this chapter are sometimes generically referred to as "prepaid," or "prepaid cards," or even the "prepaid industry," even when the cards are often reloadable and not technically prepaid. This moniker is misleading, but you'll likely see it occasionally, so don't let the generic prepaid term confuse you.

With this in mind, let's take a look at the first and arguably best option available for the delivery of rewards funding — the custom reloadable branded debit card.

Reloadable Branded Debit Card

When clients ask us what form of reward distribution to use for their incentive program, we typically start with the reloadable branded debit card. There are several reasons why. Before we go into the advantages of the reloadable branded debit card, though, let's be clear about what they are.

First, this type of card can be reused many times. Once you hand it over to a recipient, you can add money to the account repeatedly without needing to issue them a new card. This differentiates this type of card from prepaid cards (which we'll discuss in the next section).

And additionally, of course, these cards are branded. This means that your company's logo, color scheme, and more can appear directly on the card.

While the options available to you for branding will be determined by both the incentive partner and bank that you're working with, we tend to offer our customers a few options that are fairly standard across the industry. These branding options include:

- Full Custom: This type is as customized as a branded debit card can get. It includes up to four colors (full color), a custom card carrier, the brand logo, and more. Basically, anything goes within reason.

- Partial Custom: As you might imagine, full custom cards can get a bit pricey, especially if the quantities aren't large enough to see economies of scale. As a compromise between customization and cost, you can go with a partial custom debit card. These usually come with a single-color option, as well as some limitations on how and where things can be oriented on the card.

- Branded Stock/Affinity: The branded stock/affinity option is cheaper than a partial custom design. The lower price tag means more limitations, though. Essentially, the branded stock card amounts to a choice from a handful of standard designs, along with a single one-color company logo (usually in black or white).

- Non-Branded: Lastly, there's the option of a non-branded card. We never recommend this to clients, as you lose out on the brand affinity that a custom debit card can create.

There are a lot of advantages to custom reloadable debit cards. First off, there's the convenience of only having to order them once for each recipient and then simply adding funds as needed, which is convenient for you and your participant. It can also mean cost savings in the long run because you won't need to order large numbers of disposable cards over the course of years.

Additionally, branded reloadable debit cards can create major brand loyalty and affinity. Every time one of your employees or a third-party sales rep pulls out that card to use it, they're associating the pleasure and value of that purchase with your company. This may be happening subconsciously, but it's happening nonetheless. Over the course of months and years of purchases, a single branded debit card has the potential to create a massive amount of positive sentiment for your brand.

Lastly, these cards can be used anywhere that Visa or MasterCard are accepted. So rather than rewarding a participant with points that can only be redeemed for certain items, you're giving them the freedom to choose how and where they'll spend the rewards they've earned.

If there's one major downside to these debit cards, it's cost. They cost more up front, of course, particularly if you opt for the fully customized version. Particularly when compared to a single-use prepaid card, reloadable debit cards can appear a bit pricey. If you're just ordering a handful of them for your organization, the added cost will sting more. If you're looking to order thousands of them, though, the difference in expense may be negligible. Additionally, these cards cost slightly more per funding load than single-use prepaid cards do.

When weighing the relative advantages and disadvantages of a reloadable versus a prepaid debit card, remember to consider the long-term, big-picture scenario. As we've stressed, incentive programs must be consistent to work. Assume that you're committing to this form of rewards distribution for some time to come, and consider the cost of ordering replacement prepaid cards against only having to buy reloadable cards once.

Prepaid Branded Debit Card (aka Rebate Card)

These cards miss out on a couple of the advantages associated with a reloadable branded debit card, but prepaid branded debit cards remain an excellent option for distributing rewards. And in certain scenarios, they're actually a better choice, particularly when rewarding a customer as part of a rebate program. Given how ubiquitous it is to use these types of cards for this purpose, we sometimes simply refer to them as "rebate cards" rather than prepaid branded debit cards.

Traditionally, an employee's bonus, a third-party sales rep's incentive, and a customer's rebate would all simply be paid out with a standard check. There's nothing wrong with a check per se, but there's no doubt that you're missing out on all sorts of opportunities if you go this route rather than using a branded debit card of some kind.

As is the case with reloadable branded debit cards, prepaid cards give you the advantage of baked-in affinity for the user. Whether it's a third-party rep, an employee, or one of your customers, you're creating brand affinity every time the user pulls out the card to swipe it for a transaction. That's something you simply can't accomplish with a check or direct deposit.

149

Additionally, prepaid cards are easy to use and activate. The recipient can usually do it with a quick phone call or website visit, and they'll have access to their funds instantly. And just like reloadable cards, they're accepted anywhere and everywhere.

Lastly, it's worth pointing out that prepaid cards are particularly advantageous when it comes to less-frequent sales incentives. While it certainly makes sense to use this kind of card for a rebate (given that you won't be reloading a customer's card after they've used it), prepaid cards can also be a better choice for employee or third-party incentive programs that are one-off initiatives. While we do generally recommend putting programs in place for the long haul, this isn't always an option. A company that's going out of business and needs to liquidate inventory, for example, wouldn't want to opt for reloadable debit cards as part of their sales incentive program.

The only real downside to the prepaid debit card is that it's slightly less convenient for both the issuer and recipient. First, you'll need to issue a new prepaid card every time a new reward is earned. Meanwhile, users will have to activate a new card repeatedly rather than simply having the amount on the card automatically funded.

Virtual Debit Cards

If you haven't yet encountered a virtual debit card first-hand, it's likely just a matter of time until you do.

A decade ago, fears of the end of the big box store and shopping mall retail format[44] were just that: fears. Now, those fears are quickly becoming reality. The number of online retailers and the overall e-commerce retail share continues to skyrocket year over year, and the need for an actual physical debit card for making purchases decreases.

Think about it for a moment. Do you actually pull out your debit card every time you want to make a purchase online? Probably not. Instead, you probably have card numbers (and expiration dates, and maybe even security codes) saved on your phone or desktop browser. You simply allow your browser to autofill that information when you make a purchase with a new retailer. And, of course, most online retailers offer you the option of storing your card information, making it particularly easy to make repeat purchases. Amazon's one-click ordering is a particularly strong example of this sort of convenience.

So, the line of thinking goes, if in-person retail is on the decline, online retail is on the rise, and you don't actually need a physical card for making these purchases, then... why provide a physical debit card in the first place? Why not simply make debit cards virtual? And, as it turns out, the virtual debit card is an increasingly popular option for distributing rewards and rebates to employees and customers.

Our advice to clients is that this is a trend worth watching and it's worth considering the virtual debit card option. It can be particularly useful for large-scale rebate offers, where mailing out physical cards could be cost prohibitive and cumbersome. The biggest advantage for virtual debit cards (aside from their sheer convenience for the issuer) is the low-price tag that comes with them. With no physical

151

card, no printing, no postage, and no design work, the entire process will remain cheaper than issuing a physical card.

On the flip side, there's no denying that virtual debit cards aren't as popular as actual physical cards, at least not at the time of this printing. One of the major downsides is the lack of familiarity you're bound to encounter with certain users. If someone has never used a virtual debit card, the whole notion of getting their card info via email and then making purchases might confuse them. And, on top of this, there's no denying that people like to receive something they can touch and feel. Part of what you gain with the physical debit card over a simple bank transfer is the actual item itself. In the same vein, seeing an email show up in your inbox with a link to a virtual debit card just isn't the same as receiving an actual card in the mail (or in-person).

Using a virtual debit card as a reward option also reduces the potential for brand affinity. Sure, the recipient *might* think of your company when they go to use the card for an online purchase. But at the same time, you're still missing out on the opportunity to put a physical branded card with your company's logo and color scheme into the recipient's wallet. Not only will brand affinity be weaker when they're using the card—they also won't have the opportunity to passively notice your brand image each time they open their wallet.

For these reasons, we tend to see clients opting for physical cards more often than virtual debit cards. Still, though, they're worth keeping an eye on as the retail market continues to shift and change.

***

Debit cards, of course, aren't the only way to offer rewards. As we'll see in the next chapter, there's another popular option that allows you to effectively incentivize certain behaviors by employees, third parties, and customers.

Chapter 11

Merchandise and Travel

A t this point, we've looked exclusively at how to reward employees, third-party salespeople, and customers with an exclusively cash-based model. Rewarding people with cash makes sense. Everyone needs cash, right? It only makes sense that people would be happy to receive a prepaid debit card as a reward. There's no question that this form of incentive is effective, as we've seen it work wonders for many of our clients over the years.

There's no reason to simply limit your reward options to cash, though. In fact, we would argue that only offering cash incentives to your employees is a major mistake. While you might think that cash rewards would be the most desirable for recipients, the data actually shows that merchandise and travel provide greater employee satisfaction *and* lead to higher ROI.

In this chapter, we'll take a look at incorporating merchandise and travel into your incentive program, examining the relative advantages of merchandise and travel over cash, how to implement merchandise and travel into your incentive program, what items to offer, and some tips on how to leverage the power of these incentive types to their fullest. We'll also discuss how powerful these types of incentives can be when it comes to strengthening brand affinity.

Cash or Merchandise and Travel?

Before we go any further, let's address the elephant in the room. Why are merchandise and travel actually desirable when compared to cash? Does it make sense to even think about offering them?

On the one hand, there's no question that merchandise and travel rewards are more "fun" than simply receiving a debit card. A flat screen TV? A romantic Alaskan cruise? Those are exciting prospects. A debit card that you might end up using for groceries and gas? Helpful, yes. Important, yes. But fun? Not so much.

Still, conventional wisdom would dictate that the average person prefers a cash reward to a merchandise- or travel-based reward. It's understandable to be a little skeptical of how these kinds of rewards might be received by employees, especially in comparison to cash offerings. The odds are good that you self-identify as someone who would take the cash if given the option between the two. And in fact, a study conducted by Hein & Alonzo and featured in *Incentive* magazine confirms the likelihood of this.[45] When asked whether they would prefer $1,500 in cash, a travel reward worth $1,500, or a merchandise reward worth $1,500, 79% of respondents say they'd prefer the cash.

Why, then, would anyone opt to go with a merchandise and travel-focused incentive program rather than simply issuing prepaid branded debit cards to their employees? What advantage could there possibly be, especially when nearly 8 out of 10 employees clearly indicate they would just prefer cash rather than a cruise or a TV?

As we demonstrated early on in this book, incentives can be complicated. Not because of anything inherently complex about incentives, of course. In fact, we've shown time and again that incentive programs can be incredibly simple to implement. The complications arise, however, because incentives must be designed to fit with human behavior. Human behavior can be anything but straightforward.

While 79% of people might claim they prefer cash to other forms of rewards, the numbers change significantly when we look at how people actually respond once they've received the reward.

In a study published in the Journal of Economic Psychology,[46] Shaffer & Arkes presented three groups of respondents with three separate options. Each group was given the same base scenario: They're a new college graduate at an entry level job, and they're about to receive an end-of-year bonus reward. In this hypothetical scenario, only about 50% of employees are receiving the reward, as the other 50% failed to qualify.

Group 1 is told that they will be receiving a cash bonus worth $1,500 after taxes. Group 2 is given the option to choose from among 5 luxury merchandise and travel rewards, including a big screen TV, a cruise, and a top-of-the-line home audio system. Group 3 also gets to choose a reward, but is given a much more mundane, utilitarian selection, including a washer and dryer set and a one-year supply of gas. The participants in groups 2 and 3 received no mention of a cash bonus and weren't given the option of choosing cash over a tangible reward. However, they were told that each of the items on the reward list was worth approximately $1,500.

Each group was then asked to rate how satisfied there were with their bonus on a scale of 1 to 7, with 1 being extremely dissatisfied and 7 being extremely satisfied. The cash group rated their satisfaction as a 5, while groups 2 and 3 both rated their satisfaction as a 6. Groups 2 and 3 then were presented with a cash option and asked how likely they would be to choose the cash instead of the tangible reward on a scale of 1 to 7 (1 being extremely likely to choose the cash, and 7 being extremely likely to choose the merchandise or travel reward). Group 3 (the utilitarian reward group) gave an average response of 4 (meaning they had no preference between cash and merchandise or travel), group 2 responded with a median preference of 2, meaning they were very likely to choose cash over a tangible reward.

Consider for a moment what this means. Even though group 2 was measurably happier than group 1, they would still choose cash if given the option. This means that particularly when it comes to luxury rewards, people may only be more satisfied with their reward outcome if they're not also given the option of cash. If they are, they're much more likely to take the cash than the tangible reward— even though it will result in them being less satisfied than someone receiving a cruise or a new TV.

The data doesn't stop there, though. It's not just about employee preference, after all. Return on investment is important, too. So, which option results in better ROI?

Given that merchandise- and travel-reward options would seemingly be more complex to offer to employees than a simple prepaid debit card, one might conclude that the ROI for these options is bound to be lower. In fact, though, the opposite is often true.

A marketing executive at Goodyear Tire & Rubber wanted to determine which form of incentive would result in a better ROI with salespeople. He designed a sales incentive program[47] for managers and sales associates at 900 stores nationwide. The stores were then divided into two groups, with the stores evenly distributed between the two groups according to annual sales so as to ensure that data wouldn't end up skewed according to preexisting sales trends.

The sales incentive was targeted at a specific type of tire. Group 1 was given a monetary reward for every 12 of these tires they sold, while Group 2 received a merchandise or travel reward of the equivalent amount for every 12 tires sold.

The results were astonishing. Group 2 (the merchandise and travel group) outperformed Group 1 in terms of sales by a margin of 46%. And when it comes to actual return on investment, the numbers were just as staggering. The ROI for Group 2 came out to 31%, indicating that the program was well worth it for Goodyear. Meanwhile, the Group 1 ROI wasn't just less than group 2—it was actually negative. In fact, the cash incentive group ended up with an ROI of -20%. In other words, the program was a complete failure for Goodyear. (We almost never see a negative ROI scenario, so don't let this third-party case study scare you from cash incentives.)

But if you had asked these employees beforehand whether they'd prefer cash or merchandise and travel, guess what? Chances are good that about 80% of them would have responded "cash."

The bottom line here is simple: While it may be true that many employees would indicate that they'd prefer a cash reward over travel and merchandise, the reality is that the latter can result in better employee satisfaction, better sales, and better ROI. Without a doubt, there's a strong argument to be made for offering merchandise and travel rewards to your employees.

How to Implement Merchandise and Travel Programs

After seeing those numbers, you might be eager to get started with merchandise and travel options for your company's incentive program. But if you've never done it before, the whole prospect can feel a little overwhelming.

First, you'll want to set up an online portal. Just as with any other incentives option, you'll want to ensure that your portal is customized and branded specific to your needs. This is where your employees will log in to claim their rewards, and it's a good opportunity to reinforce and strengthen brand affinity.

A popular way of formatting an online merchandise and travel rewards portal involves using a points system. Rather than receiving cash in exchange for meeting a specific outcome, employees get a certain number of points. These points can then be accumulated and redeemed via the web portal. Aside from being fun—everyone loves to rack up points—this is also a helpful way to discourage your employees from thinking in terms of cash. Remember, people will *think* that they'd prefer cash, and that it would make them happier than a merchandise or travel reward (even though it wouldn't, on average).

Your online portal can be regularly updated by your incentives provider. This can happen on an annual or quarterly basis, or even monthly. The addition of new merchandise or travel packages to your online portal makes for the perfect opportunity to remind employees about the program and get them excited about new reward options. Plus, when it comes to electronics and technology, if you aren't regularly updating your options, they'll quickly become outdated and undesirable.

Aside from giving your employees the ability to rack up points and exchange them for rewards, there are other options available to you. One popular approach involves offering periodic merchandise- or travel-based bonuses.

This can take the form of a monthly drawing that all employees stand a chance of winning, or a quarterly bonus for your top sales performer. Whether you decide to structure this bonus reward as monthly, quarterly, or even annually, and regardless of whether it's merit-based or purely a matter of luck, the idea is the same. Your aim is to give employees an additional chance to win and keep the rewards program fresh with tangible prizes they can visualize. We've often seen this exact approach as extremely effective in combination with a traditional cash-based program.

What to Offer

So, you're ready to set up an online portal. You've potentially found an incentives provider. And you want to get things rolling. But what exactly are you going to offer as rewards? What tangible items will you make available in your web portal?

We've been managing these types of programs for years, and here are the items that consistently perform the best for our clients (in no specific order):

- Tablets and smartphones
- Home theater systems
- Small appliances
- Fitness and sports equipment
- Jewelry and watches
- Housewares
- Laptops and computers

This short list is far from exhaustive, though. Your company's employee demographics should dictate what you offer. If an item proves to be unpopular with employees, consider swapping it for something else. And, of course, it never hurts to get feedback from your employees and channel partners on what sorts of items they'd be excited to receive.

When it comes to travel, you want your getaway options to be all-inclusive. This means airfare, hotels, event tickets, and so on. Often, we even suggest including a prepaid debit card to handle incidentals. The following is a short list of the most popular travel packages that we've seen (in no specific order):

- New York City
- Asheville, NC
- Las Vegas, NV
- Miami, FL
- Napa Valley
- San Francisco
- Alaskan cruise
- The Masters
- The Super Bowl
- Golf Resorts in CA or FL
- Disney World

As with the merchandise above, this list isn't meant to be exhaustive. You can tailor your destinations and travel options to your employee demographics, as well as what part of the country (or world) you're in.

If you're thinking of incorporating monthly or quarterly giveaways into your merchandise and rewards incentives plan, there are a couple options available to you. If you're running a relatively small company and have a limited budget, these giveaways can be relatively inexpensive items. This option might also make sense if you opt to offer a monthly bonus or giveaway, as the sheer frequency of the offering might make high-dollar items unaffordable.

That being said, we've seen our clients achieve greater success with a combination of lower-frequency giveaways and higher-value items. It can be difficult to get your employees excited about a low-ticket item. However, you'll find that there's a certain amount of natural anticipation and office chatter that will form around a bigger giveaway. It makes sense, then, to at least consider the possibility of giving away a more expensive item on an infrequent basis, rather than regularly offering things like low-value gift cards.

In the past, our clients have had success with the following giveaway items (in no particular order):

- Big screen TVs
- Large appliance packages
- Build-your-own electronics packages
- Caribbean cruises
- Design-your-own dream vacation packages
- Prepaid debit cards (seriously)

164

Typically, we'll design a standard online catalogue of anywhere from 25 to 50 items and getaway options for our clients. Less is more. For example, it's better to have the best 65" TV rather than three different 65" TVs of varying quality.

Additionally, you'll likely find that certain items are a major hit with your participants while others fall flat. That's to be expected and shouldn't be any cause for worry. As mentioned earlier, you should be updating your product and travel offerings annually, quarterly, or even monthly. Always remember that your catalog isn't set in stone, and don't be afraid to swap out new items for those that are unpopular within your company. Your goal is to generate excitement and ultimately to change employee behavior—and you can't do that with merchandise and travel options that no one's interested in.

Inspiring Photos and Testimonials

In our experience, one of the most powerful and useful aspects of offering merchandise and travel to employees is the opportunity for photos and testimonials.

When you reward your employees strictly with prepaid debit cards, you'll rarely have an employee come tell you about an experience that the debit card made possible. Sure, maybe they used it the other night when they went out to dinner—but they're probably not going to take pictures of their meal and show you the next day. (Unless they're young and you happen to follow them on social media.)

But it's completely standard behavior for someone to snap a ton of pictures on their cruise, take selfies while on vacation in New York, or even post a quick photo of their new high definition audio system on social media. Particularly when it comes to travel, you can leverage your employees' positive experiences as a means of further incentivizing other employees.

This can take many forms. One option is to incorporate a photo gallery into your web portal that highlights past vacations taken by participants who earned travel package rewards. Another highly effective approach is to include a brief written testimonial and a picture or two from an employee in your company's email newsletter. This gives you a chance to plug your rewards program in a very tangible way. It's likely to spark conversation between your employees, and anyone who's won such a trip will effectively be doing your program promotion for you. When it comes to merchandise and travel incentive programs, satisfied employees are often your best form of advertising.

Brand Affinity

In the same vein, merchandise and travel can create affinity for your brand or company like nothing else. This is especially true when it comes to travel offerings.

To maximize the potential reward when it comes to increasing brand affinity, it's important to include spouses, partners, and families as part of your travel reward offerings. This provides the opportunity to demonstrate to both your participants and their families that you value their relationships and collective well-being. You're going out of your way to facilitate an experience that will create lasting family memories. Your participants' spouses/partners also will quickly become fans and lifelong supporters of your company and brand, even as your participants' brand affinity grows as a result of the trip.

Even more so than with a prepaid debit card, merchandise and travel will keep your brand top of mind for your employees and their family members. Every time one of them tells a story about a trip they took, they'll associate the positive experience with your brand. And when someone asks how they managed the trip or why they decided to take it, they'll likely mention your company in a positive light. The same goes for showing off a merchandise reward to friends. When the neighbors come over to watch the game on Sunday, your company will be credited for the new widescreen TV hanging on the wall.

***

For all this talk of merchandise and travel, though, it does still make sense to include cash rewards as part of your incentive program. We often recommend our clients consider a mix of both cash and merchandise/travel rewards, as prepaid debit cards are easy, affordable, and highly effective incentives offerings. Before you can implement a cash-based incentive program, though, you have to find a bank that will work with you. In the following chapter, we'll discuss what to look for in a bank—and what to avoid.

Chapter 12

What to Look for (and Avoid) in a Bank

Throughout this book, we've made the case for setting up an incentive program for your employees. To make that happen, though, you'll have to put some logistics in place ahead of time, so we'll now move on to the importance of having a web portal, the necessity of working with an outside provider, and how to design a program from the top down.

Before you can think about any of these things, there's one important aspect that you'll need to sort out. Simply put, you can't run a cash-based incentive program without a banking partner, and finding a good banking partner isn't always easy. We've had our fair share of negative experiences with banks over the years, and we hope that you'll be able to learn from our mistakes. Before we get to that, though, let's talk banks and incentives.

Banks and Incentives

First things first: Most banks don't offer custom prepaid and reloadable debit cards. And if they do, they typically don't offer them for the purposes of offering an incentive program. Sure, there are quite a few options such as American Express gift cards. And if you're a very small company that isn't planning to set up a web portal and doesn't have the resources to commit to a long-term incentive program, simply ordering some Amex gift cards could be an option.

But as we've stated earlier in this book, it's important to go all-in with an incentive program; it's not something you should half-commit to. And we'll discuss shortly, we believe web portals to be wholly necessary if you want to maximize the potential of your program. Plus, if you think an incentive program isn't in your budget, consider its relative effectiveness over and above other traditional approaches to marketing and sales as outlined in Chapter 4.

In other words, you'll want to find a bank that can actually partner with you in providing prepaid and/or reloadable debit cards. A handful of Amex gift cards isn't going to cut it.

Surprisingly, the vast majority of banks both large and small have completely ignored this space. This isn't a bad thing, but it does mean that you shouldn't waste your time calling around to your own financial institutions and existing banking partners to see whether they offer a prepaid card program. Chances are good that they won't. Instead, you'll need to search specifically for a bank that offers these sorts of services, either online or through your existing network.

It's also worth pointing out that among the banks that will act as the processor or bank of record for these sorts of transactions, many aren't going to want to work directly with you. This is also completely fine, and totally normal. Remember, banks are good at numbers, but they're often not so great when it comes to sales and marketing. It's pretty standard for you to need a go-between in the form of an incentive provider, which is something we'll discuss in an upcoming chapter.

What to Look For in a Bank

All of that begs the question, though, of what to look for when searching for a new bank. We're of the strong opinion that the most important thing to look for in a bank is experience and strong references. Find out exactly how long a bank has been offering these services, how long it's been around, and how many clients it's worked with. Then, take the time to actually call these clients and ask them about their experiences. Don't just take the bank at its word.

Remember, too, that banks change names frequently with mergers and acquisitions rampant in the banking world. So, the fact that a bank recently underwent a rebranding doesn't necessarily mean there's something potentially suspect about that bank. It's quite common for both people and processes at your preferred banking partner to remain constant, even while its name may change on a regular basis.

What to Avoid in a Bank: A Cautionary Tale

To some extent, the best way to know what to look for in a bank is by understanding what to avoid.

Over the years, we've run across our fair share of duplicitous, unscrupulous "banks." Unfortunately, there are a lot of scams out there — and also a lot of banks that are simply poorly managed and about to bite the dust, although they give no outward indications of this.

In our many experiences working with a wide variety of banks, we've encountered three situations in particular that caused great alarm for us and our partners. We're opting to share these stories with you here as a kind of cautionary tale. We've had to learn from our mistakes the hard way, but we hope that you can avoid making them in the first place.

Here are three scenarios that we've encountered. The first two caused us quite a bit of trouble, and the third is representative of us finally learning our lesson when it comes to dealing with a new banking partner.

1) The Bait and Switch

Early on in our company's history, we worked with a small banking partner who claimed that they could produce a very small batch of custom, prepaid debit cards. Larger banks were unwilling to fulfill such a relatively small order, so we opted to go with this smaller bank.

At the 11th hour, we received a call informing us that the cards could no longer be custom. Instead, we'd have to use generic, unbranded cards. We had already launched the program, so it was too late to pull out. We begrudgingly accepted the generic cards, assuming that things would at least go smoothly from there.

Unfortunately, the situation deteriorated even further. After launching the program and distributing the generic cards, we discovered that our issuing partner had entered bankruptcy protection, meaning all the funds available on the cards would be removed if they weren't used within a specific period of time. This was all contrary to our original agreement.

With enough legal pressure, we were able to arrive at a settlement with the bank in question that effectively limited the amount we ultimately lost. We were able to achieve damage control here, but the situation was nearly catastrophic.

The lesson here? If something sounds too good to be true, it probably is.

2) The Lack of References

Years ago, a prospective client reached out to us about a potential partnership. They were interested in a General Purpose Reloadable (GPR) card program, though, which was something we didn't offer at the time.

At about this same time, we met a banking partner through our network who claimed to offer a GPR program. We were a little uneasy, as this person had no website and no official internet presence. But we opted to make the introduction anyway as a favor to the prospective client. We figured that we had met them through our network, and it was ultimately up to the prospect who had originally contacted us to vet them before agreeing to work with them.

Long story short, things didn't go well. The company in question ended up defrauding two separate firms — the one which had originally contacted us, plus another firm — out of approximately $25,000 each. We and the firms in question all chose to look past the complete lack of experience, references, and web presence. We weren't directly responsible for the outcome, but we had to acknowledge that we'd been the ones to make the introduction. Our reputation was somewhat tarnished, and it took us time to recover emotionally from the fraud.

The lesson here? Always check references. If a bank gives you even the slightest sense that something's off, walk away from the deal.

3) The Disappearing Bank

When you first start out in many industries, particularly in the business-to-business (B2B) space, it's common to spend some time doing cold calls and other forms of outreach. This is a necessary evil when you're first trying to get off the ground. But if you're good at what you do, you shouldn't have to keep this up for long. Before you know it, your reputation leads to a steady stream of incoming business.

In other words, B2B companies that are good at what they do shouldn't be spending a ton of time on cold calls to new prospects. Some time ago, after the two experiences mentioned above, a new bank reached out to us and requested a meeting, claiming to offer prepaid and reloadable debit card services that would mesh well with what many of our clients needed.

Rather than jumping at the offer for a meeting, we instinctively asked for references. And guess what? We never received them. When we attempted to check back sometime later, the company had fallen off the face of the earth. Obviously, they weren't up to the task. In learning from our past mistakes, we were able to avoid a repeat scenario with an unstable and/or fraudulent bank.

We don't mean to paint a wholly negative picture by mentioning these unpleasant experiences. We've found a number of banking partners that are reputable, financially strong, and great at what they do. If you look hard enough, you'll be able to do the same.

You've probably noticed that pricing hasn't come up in this chapter at all. We'll discuss pricing a little later, but for now, it's critical to separate pricing from financial stability. They're mutually exclusive, and while you can absolutely find good value AND a great reputation in the same banking partner, it's important to not become blinded by rock-bottom prices.

There are plenty of solid banking partners out there, but it pays to be picky in your search. Don't jump at the first option you find. Do your homework, call their references, and choose a bank that has a proven track record.

***

With the right banking partner lined up, you can begin to think about high-level design for your incentive program. In the next chapter, we'll look at how to plan out your program prior to launch, including how to develop a budget, set goals, measure and determine ROI, and more.

Chapter 13

How to Design an Incentive program

Congratulations! You're now ready to plan your first incentive program at a high level.

As you approach the task, we can't stress this enough: Proper planning is absolutely essential to the success of an incentive program. If you don't take the time to put together a high-level plan for your entire program, including goals, timelines, expectations, and more, the odds of achieving your intended outcomes are significantly diminished.

With that in mind, let's walk you through each of the most important items to consider when it comes to designing your incentive program: How to identify key players, clarify your goals, set reasonable expectations, get bank approval, and put together a realistic timeline. Then you'll be ready to jump in and start planning your first program.

Identifying the Players

Your first step should be identifying the key players that will be involved with your program. You'll also want to identify the level that they operate at within their company—whether it's your organization or an independent distributor.

What do we mean when we say, "key players?" Here are just a few examples:

- Salespeople at dealerships

- Dealer sales managers

- Employees

- District managers

- Corporate managers

- Global administrators

- Anyone involved in design approval or the decision-making process

It's essential that you take the time to put together this list for yourself. It will likely include a few players from the short list above, a few different ones. This list could include the end-user of the program, the managers who will need to educate their departments on how the program works, or upper level management who will be reviewing the program each step of the way to approve designs and costs. You'll want to take the time to map them all out. By having a bird's eye view of these various players in place from the beginning, you'll have a better sense of how complex the program's execution will actually be. Identifying this ahead of time can save you a lot of aggravation later.

Identifying Your Goals

Once you know who the key players in your incentive program will be, it's time to identify your goals.

Simply put, every successful incentive program starts with clearly identifying and understanding your goals. Without a well-defined goal, your program can't succeed by definition. How will you determine how to measure ROI without a goal? How will you know that you've accomplished what you set out to do if you don't have a clear, measurable goal from the start?

Throughout this book, we've discussed a wide variety of potential goals for a properly designed incentive program. Some of the major highlights include:

- Increase in overall sales
- Increase in total profit
- Increase in sales of particular product(s) or segment(s) of a business
- Improved customer retention
- Improved customer satisfaction
- Rewarding customer loyalty
- Changes in salesperson behavior
- Changes in employee behavior

It's perfectly possible to achieve more than one of these goals with a single program and this is an important fact to keep in mind. There's no need to assume that you can only increase total profit, or that a particular incentive program can only focus on changing employee behavior without having an impact on customer retention. If you take another look at the list of goals above, you'll see that many of them are closely related. By identifying your goals ahead of time, you can design a program that's well suited to achieving each and every one of them.

Setting Expectations

Once your goals have been set and you know the key players who will be involved in your incentive program, it's time to set your expectations. Remember: Rome wasn't built in a day. The same is true for your incentive program. You won't be able to design and implement a program today, or tomorrow, or even by next week. It's going to take some time.

Setting reasonable expectations is important for a couple of reasons. First, you don't want to get discouraged midway through the process because of expectations that are beyond what's practical. By knowing what's achievable and what's not, you can evaluate how your design and launch are progressing in a way that's constructive. Additionally, you want to ensure that the other decision makers at your organization are on the same page. If they expect your program to be ready to go two weeks from now, they're likely to end up pretty disappointed when it doesn't launch for months.

Generally speaking, the development of a solid incentive program should take anywhere from eight weeks in the best-case scenario to as much as 26 weeks (six months) in the worst-case scenario. These are both extreme examples, though. In our experience, the average development time we've seen from start to finish tends to be about 12 to 16 weeks.

What determines these development times? There are two factors that can increase lead time significantly that you have limited control over.

First, if you're opting to use a fully custom debit card of some kind, expect the actual approval of your design to take time. The powers-that-be at Visa or Mastercard will need to approve your card before it can be issued, and this can result in a significant delay. This means that the sooner your design is submitted for approval, the sooner you'll be able to launch your program.

Additionally, those opting to use a web portal must devote a significant amount of time to web portal design and functioning. This can be a complex process involving multiple rounds of feedback and revisions. Web portals can indeed be time consuming, but we highly recommend them for the vast majority of our clients as you'll see in the next chapter.

Keep in mind that it is possible to speed up launch time, even if you're using a debit card. If you're in a serious hurry, one option involves using a simple branded stock/ affinity card rather than a fully customizable debit card option. Affinity cards are generic but aesthetically pleasing debit cards, typically with the ability to add a single-color version of your logo (usually in black or white) for some degree of customization.

While affinity cards certainly don't provide the same level of customization or potential brand affinity (ironically) as a fully customizable debit card since they just aren't as striking as a multi-color, custom card featuring your company's color logo, they offer two major advantages. First, they're often significantly cheaper for smaller programs; and second, the approval process for these types of cards is much faster. However, considering the relative disadvantages associated with limited customization, we generally only recommend these types of cards to clients where both cost and time are of major concern.

Creating a Timeline

As part of setting reasonable expectations for your program, you'll want to put together a timeline that takes into account all of your major milestones and program goals.

We can't stress enough just how important a well thought out timeline is for any program to be successful. There are numerous reasons why a proper timeline is so important:

1. **SETTING EXPECTATIONS**: A good timeline sets realistic expectations for everyone at your company, particularly the upper-level, key players you might have to answer to throughout the process.

2. **ACCOUNTABILITY**: A timeline allows you to hold other people accountable. If there are definitive dates and deadlines in place, you'll know exactly where you stand from week to week.

3. **AVOIDING CONFLICTS**: By putting together a time-line in advance, you'll be able to avoid potential scheduling conflicts (other projects, holidays, and so on).

4. **MEASURING SUCCESS**: Particularly when you're putting together a complex, large-scale program, it's important to be able to check in with your team periodically and see how things are progressing. With a definitive schedule in place, you'll be able to point to whether things are going according to plan or if adjustments need to be made.

One of the most important things to keep in mind is the sheer scope and scale of your project. Particularly with larger organizations, it's essential to remember that there will be a whole host of expectations held by the various key players involved in the process. Your incentive program isn't being created in a vacuum, after all. By laying out a timeline, you can ensure that everyone's expectations are more or less aligned, and that these key players understand what their responsibilities, roles, and accompanying deadlines look like.

Some of the most important milestones and accompanying responsibilities associated with an incentive program might include:

- **CARD DESIGN**: In addition to designing the card itself, you'll need to obtain design approval before it can be sent off to Visa or Mastercard. They'll then have to approve the design, too.

- **BANK APPROVAL**: Getting approved by a bank can be a lengthy process, and one which will likely involve the collaboration of others at your organization to assemble revenue figures, answer questions about ownership structure, and so on. See the section below for more detail.

- **WEB PORTAL**: Your incentive partner will likely work with you on your web portal, and you'll probably need to obtain feedback and revision approval from others in your organization.

- **PROGRAM RULES**: Putting together the rules for your incentive program will likely be a collaborative process and can involve multiple rounds of revision and input.

- **TERMS & CONDITIONS (T&C)**: The same goes for your program's terms & conditions, these will likely be created with input from multiple parties, which can take a significant amount of time.

- **TESTING**: You should never launch an incentive program without properly testing it first. Be sure to allow time toward the end of your proposed launch calendar for adequate program testing.

You'll likely need to add more items to this list that'll be specific to your organization and situation. Remember, a detailed timeline is one of your most valuable tools when it comes to designing and launching your program.

Getting Approved by a Bank

Once your timeline is in place, you'll quickly arrive at a very important step: Getting your program approved by a bank, a process that's often a lengthy one. Following the financial crisis of 2008, however, today it's an even more time-consuming ordeal. Banks are now inclined to take extra time to get to know each of their clients before moving forward with an incentive program. They'll want to get a complete picture of your business dealings before agreeing to work with you.

There are two things going on here. First, the bank wants to ensure that they're not putting themselves at risk in the post-recession economy. And just as importantly, the bank is checking to ensure that there's nothing illegal or otherwise unethical occurring within your organization. This latter point particularly comes into play for certain business types. If you're running a marijuana-based business, a gambling institution, or a business with overseas ownership based in a country that's not traditionally considered to be allied with U.S. interests, you can expect additional scrutiny.

Be prepared to fill out various documents with a range of questions about your organization that may include your organization's ownership structure, rules for doing business, and overall revenue history and projections, along with questions regarding the purpose and intention of your incentive program. If your company is privately held, you can typically provide general revenue numbers rather than specifics. Why would the bank be doing this? They want to ensure that they've put in the time for due diligence and are making an informed decision. Additionally, though, they may be looking to determine whether the resources associated with the initial setup for your program will be worth their trouble from a profit standpoint.

185

The result of this is that startups will generally have a harder time getting approval for certain types of programs, particularly reloadable rewards card. This is obviously less true for startups that are particularly well-funded. Single use rebate cards are much easier to get approved; but, as we discussed in the customer rewards chapter, single use rebate cards aren't ideal for certain incentive programs and goals.

There's some good news here, though. Even if your company is a new startup or a smaller organization, you can still qualify for more complex programs with the help of a good full-service management partner. (We'll discuss management partners in further detail later in the book.) For example, it's not uncommon for banks to have a $1 million annual minimum issuance rule—something that's unrealistic for smaller businesses. With a larger partner, though, it's possible to have this minimum reduced. There are two factors at play here. First, the bank will assume that your partner has ostensibly done its own due diligence and is backing you for a reason (i.e., because your program represents a good opportunity). And second, the bank will look at all the business they're currently doing with your partner organization and take it into consideration as part of their decision making. There's a certain amount of opportunity cost involved here, as the bank will risk losing your larger partner organization if another bank opts to take the deal instead.

A Note on Banks and Breakage

In Chapter 8, we briefly discussed breakage in relation to rebates. You'll recall that in the example of a customer rebate program, breakage refers to the number of people who fail to redeem the rebate offer that's presented to them. Breakage rates as high as 50% are not uncommon in such programs.

When it comes to setting up a debit card-based program with a bank, you might be wondering if breakage is something to take into account. The answer depends on both the bank you're working with and the specifics of your program.

Consider that of all of the cards you distribute—whether prepaid or reloadable—some amount of the funds on those cards will never actually be spent. With this in mind, you might be tempted to broach the topic of breakage with your bank. After all, shouldn't you be able to negotiate a better deal considering the funds that will never even leave the bank's accounts?

In reality, the vast majority of banks won't want to get into a discussion of breakage. That's because with most debit card programs, breakage is already factored into the upfront pricing you're offered. The bank considers this breakage to be part of their business model, and therefore determines their rates based on the assumption that they'll end up keeping a certain amount of money that your program participants never actually get around to spending.

Some banks will indeed consider splitting the breakage with you, but this approach comes with some risks. First of all, there's no question that your program's up-front pricing will increase as a result. You'll likely see increases in card costs, postage rates, reload fees, and so on.

Secondly, breakage isn't something that happens right away. Depending on the expiration date of the cards you issue, it could take two to three years before you really start to see results from breakage. In other words, breakage is a long game. Finally, breakage can pose problems for your organization's finance and treasury departments. How should this money be treated? How should the collection take place? What type of income would this be considered?

Considering the added risks, costs, workload, and time-line, we generally recommend that our clients avoid trying to cash-in on breakage. It is an option with certain banks, however.

***

You now have the tools that you need to start designing your program. In the next chapter, we'll take a look at one of the most important milestones mentioned above: Developing a web portal.

Chapter 14

Do I Need a Web Portal?

O ver the years, we've worked with a wide range of clients in devising and implementing incentive programs. These clients have come from a diverse range of industries and niches, and their program needs and strategies have varied widely. But one question that we get all the time from our clients, no matter how different they may be from one another, is: Do I need a program web portal?

In a word, yes. You do need a program web portal.

The best incentive programs will have a website of some kind associated with them. There's no question that having a web portal will make your life easier in the long run, along with giving your incentive program added authority and clout. Web portals look professional, plain and simple, and they make things easier for your program participants.

So let's take a deeper dive into why you really need a web portal, looking at the benefits, the notion of integrating it with your existing internet presence, and the possibility of incorporating a mobile app into your digital presence. Lastly, we'll examine the handful of scenarios where a web portal isn't as necessary.

Benefits of Having a Web Portal

Aside from the added authority that a professional looking site will give your program, there are three primary benefits that we like to point out to our clients. First, having a web portal allows you to consolidate everything about your incentive program into one place. This includes things like:

- **PROGRAM RULES AND OFFERS**: It's essential that program participants understand the rules of your program as well as the eligible offers. A web portal is the perfect place to host all of this information.

- **ENTRY FORMS AND DATA COLLECTION**: Regardless of whether you're running an employee incentive program, a program targeted at independent sales-people, or a customer loyalty or rebate program, you'll often need to collect data from program participants. Doing so with a web portal keeps everything in one place and makes data collection easy.

- **PROGRESS AND BALANCES:** Your program participants will want to be able to check in and see how they're doing. Have they accumulated enough points to redeem their desired reward? What's the balance of their reloadable debit card? A web portal gives your participants a place to do this on their own, rather than calling you with questions.

Next, a web portal provides you with a place to host your program's terms and conditions at next to no cost, and be able to update your terms and conditions as needed. Just imagine how expensive and time consuming it would be to send out a paper copy of your terms and conditions to all program participants if you need to make a minor change or update—that's potentially thousands upon thousands of pieces of mail. With a web portal, updating your terms and conditions is simple, fast, and cheap. By making the website the absolute authority on the current T&C's, there is no question where things stand.

Most importantly of all, though, a web portal will allow you to automate virtually everything about your program. Amongst other things, this includes:

- **POINT TABULATIONS:** Attempting to keep track of program participant points without a web portal can make for a complex task. A properly coded website takes care of this process for you automatically.

- **USER APPROVAL:** Whether it's approving new participant signups or fulfilling orders for merchandise or travel, approving user requests with less work is one of the greatest advantages of having a web portal.

- **PASSWORD RETRIEVAL:** With automatic password retrieval, you'll dramatically cut back on the number of phone calls and support emails you receive.

- **PARTICIPANT SUPPORT:** Setting up a frequently asked questions and/or a help section on your site creates an automated support option for users, thus reducing the number of support requests coming in.

There's no question. A web portal offers unparalleled benefits for your incentive program.

Integration with Existing User Portals

Once a client has acknowledged that a web portal is a good idea, there's often a common follow-up question: Can the rewards portal integrate with their existing user portal and web presence?

Technically speaking, yes. There's typically no reason from an IT perspective that you *can't* integrate your rewards web portal with an existing user portal on your website. That said, though, we generally don't recommend it for a couple of reasons.

Attempting to integrate your rewards web presence with an existing user portal is almost certainly going to cost you more. You'll need to either involve your own IT department or a third-party firm to assist with the required programming. And, in 99% of cases, neither your IT department nor the hypothetical third-party will have any experience with developing portals for incentive programs. This means that the learning curve will undoubtedly be quite high. As a result, your ROI will start to fall off rather quickly. If you run the numbers, you're likely to find that integration simply isn't worth it.

It's also important to remember that whether you're talking about employees or channel partners, the registration process will need to include the collection of personal data from users. More often than not, some of the data required will differ from the personal data that's already

192

stored as part of your existing user portal. This means that you end up needing to collect additional data either way, which adds another layer of complexity to any attempt to integrate your rewards web portal with an existing user portal.

For these reasons, we generally recommend keeping your rewards portal separate from your existing web presence. That said, though, there's a viable solution available that can serve as something of a compromise between fully integrating your web portals on the one hand and keeping them wholly separate on the other: Single sign on, or SSO.

Single-sign-on Web Portals

If you already have another intranet or extranet web portal (meaning it either lives on an internal network or an external network with access controls), arguably the best solution when setting up your rewards site involves leveraging what's called single sign on, or SSO. Using SSO will simplify things for your users, which will ultimately make things simpler for you (meaning less phone calls and support emails to respond to).

By creating an SSO for users, your program participants will be able to use the same username and password credentials to sign in to both your existing web portal and your new rewards site. SSO allows for quick deployment of a proven rewards platform with the right functionality, all while keeping things as easy as possible for the end user. SSO rules can even be programmed to identify first-time users, thus allowing you to collect personal data as needed for payment records. That user profile is then permanently linked to both web presences, making future access a snap.

If you opt not to use SSO, it's essential that you incorporate automatic password retrieval into your design. Your program participants will inevitably confuse their two accounts. When they do, they'll be calling and emailing you for password retrieval help. By automating this process, you can free up your phone lines and email inbox.

Do I Need a Mobile App?

Once a client has accepted that they need a web portal, with or without SSO, we often get the same follow up question from them: Do I need a mobile app, too?

The short answer is no, you probably don't need a mobile app. It's not going to be a requirement in most client scenarios.

Why? Giving your program participants access to a mobile app is going to be significantly more complicated than simply launching a mobile responsive website, with little in the way of additional benefits. Developing an app, especially a native app, on top of an online portal is going to increase your costs considerably. For one thing, there are differences in iOS and Android from a development perspective, which means that you'll essentially need to build out two apps (as only offering one or the other isn't realistic). While new development tools do allow programmers to create the code once and then publish separately for iOS and Android, it's not foolproof, and still requires maintaining publisher accounts with both platforms.

Additionally, you'll have the added costs associated with ongoing testing and maintenance, both leading up to and following the launch of your app. This kind of testing and maintenance is important to ensure that your app actually works, and it can get expensive quickly. Finally, don't forget that Apple and Google might want a cut of the action on your financial transactions, as they can often take up to 25% of all transactions. While incentive and rebate programs *should* fall outside of the normal realm of app store profit share, it might cause an issue depending on your program's specific rules.

In our experience, an app makes the most sense for a client when they have a strong need to offer program participants a particular kind of functionality that's only really possible with a mobile phone. One example of this would be taking a photo of something so that it can be uploaded to their user account for processing (although this is technically available in a less convenient form without an app). Another example might involve a scenario where users need to be able to store documents from the web portal on their local device, in which case an app would make mobile access to those documents easier.

We should add, too, that some clients want to add an app to their offerings simply because they want to be able to say that they have an app. This is understandable, and there's nothing wrong with this per se. Also, apps will allow you to issue push notifications directly to users' devices, which could occasionally be of value. Just take into account the costs associated with adding an app and understand that they will likely cut into your ROI.

When Do I Not Need a Web Portal?

We hope we've convinced you of just how important official program websites are for your program. But we would be remiss if we didn't address one last question: When do I *not* need a web portal? There are in fact a couple of situations where web portals aren't necessary, and we want to be sure to address those.

If you're looking to offer a simple, straightforward, one-time reward or rebate of some kind—meaning that offering this reward or rebate requires little to no collection or storage of electronic data—then an online web portal may be overkill. Of course, as we've mentioned throughout this book, the most effective incentive programs involve long-term commitments, whether they're targeted at customers or employees. Generally speaking, we don't recommend short-term programs with no room for expansion or continuation, which is one of the reasons why we tend to tell our clients that a web portal is almost mandatory. But, if you have a good reason to offer a one-time program to your employees or customers, you can likely do it without a web portal.

When it comes to rebate programs, we've seen some companies that opt to stick to physical mail for rebate redemption. Oftentimes, companies will do this intentionally to increase breakage, or the number of customers who fail to follow through with the rebate process. Requiring customers to submit a physical form in the mail can certainly discourage them from participating, particularly as sending snail mail becomes less popular. If you're taking this approach, then a web portal is unlikely to be necessary.

Lastly, we'll sometimes see clients who opt to communicate rewards through traditional media and then complete their reward offers via mail or in-person. In these sorts of circumstances, there's no real benefit to creating a web portal.

***

At this point, you're likely ready to add the tasks associated with building out a web portal to your launch schedule. Before you can move forward, though, there's one big thing that needs to be addressed: Working with an outside management partner. Is working with an external firm necessary? And, if so, what should you look for? We'll answer these questions, and more, in the next chapter.

Chapter 15

Working with a Management Partner

By now, you've been exposed to a huge amount of information when it comes to creating an incentive program. You know why incentives are important, how to design a program of your own, and the nuts and bolts of running programs targeted at both employees and customers. But before you launch a program on your own, you've got one last question. Is it worth working with an outside firm? Would it be better to outsource some (or all) of this work, rather than try to do everything in-house?

In this chapter, we'll take a detailed look at what it means to work with an incentives firm. We'll discuss the major advantages of contracting an outside agency, along with what to look for when you're shopping around. Let's get started.

Should I Hire an Outside Firm?

It's important to highlight that management partners are not banks. Banks and similar financial institutions won't offer turnkey management of your programs. They might offer a way to pull reports and submit simple payment files, but their services are narrowly focused on the debit cards themselves. There are no custom web portals, no SSO, no program customer service, no submission validation, no consulting, no marketing assistance, etc. In fact, typically your management partner will find the right bank for your needs, and handle that banking relationship on your behalf as a part of their services.

Now that you understand the differences between a management partner and a bank, should you hire an outside management partner? In a word, yes. You need an outside firm to serve as Program HQ, and to provide you with the wide array of services necessary for the success of an incentive program. Of course, it may be the case that you have a team of people on staff who could run an incentive program themselves. You may have employees who understand the best practices outlined in this book, who have the experience necessary to make it work, and who have the time in their schedules to dedicate to the program. If so, go for it. But the reality is that the vast majority—and we really do mean the *vast* majority—of businesses simply don't have the people and resources to run a successful incentive program in house. And even when they do, it's usually much more expensive and troublesome to try to run a program internally.

This is true for a number of reasons.

First, there's the learning curve. It's unlikely that you have a team of employees who have run dozens of incentive programs in the past. The learning curve is steep, as a good incentive program will involve a lot of moving parts, from the initial planning stages to the achievement of your goals. Considering how complex these programs tend to be, trying to pass them off to your internal team can result in major issues.

Next is the issue of added cost. When you actually crunch the numbers of running a program in-house versus outsourcing it to a partner, you might be surprised to see just how much more expensive it is to try and run the program yourself. A large part of this is often due to higher internal labor costs. A good outside firm will have all of the pieces in place ahead of time, and they've likely already achieved certain economies of scale with labor costs down as low as they can go. Even if they're compensating their employees comparably to yours on a per-hour basis—in fact, even if they're paying them more—the speed and efficiency with which they'll be able to accomplish tasks generally translates to a significant decrease in labor costs. Those savings can be passed on to you.

Finally, you have to consider your internal team's lack of experience handling a variety of issues. There are a lot of problems and complications that are likely to emerge when launching your first incentive program. Even after reading this book, anticipating all of them ahead of time is next to impossible. Attempting to handle everything in-house means that you'll be on your own when things do go wrong, and your lack of experience will make handling various issues more difficult.

Still not convinced that working with an outside firm is the way to go? We understand. The idea of keeping things in-house can be appealing, as it means you'll have some degree of added control over the program. But, consider all of the various roles that you'll require to run an incentive program. At a very minimum, every incentive program needs:

- **SALES:** You'll need someone on your team who's sales-focused. This person has to understand the products that you're looking to incentivize, along with the types of incentives that will yield the best results for those products. This requires incentive-specific experience.

- **CREATIVE:** You'll also need to have a creative person to handle branding the program and all of its various elements, along with things like graphic design and web portal visuals.

- **NUMBERS:** Every incentive program needs a number cruncher, or analyst. They're essential when it comes to determining the best incentive amounts to offer, whether you're talking about customer rebates or employee rewards.

- **ADMINISTRATIVE:** Without an administrative staff in place, you won't be able to audit your program along the way for reports and data extraction. Having the right administrative people ready to go is incredibly important.

- **CUSTOMER SERVICE:** Of course, we can't forget about customer service. Even the smallest of programs will have to field participant inquiries. If your program is sizeable, you'll need to be prepared for a ton of phone calls and emails. You need a customer service team in place that can handle these communications with authority and grace. Attempting to throw together a couple of people to respond to emails at the last minute isn't a great option.

- **TECHNICAL:** Finally, you'll need a developer, or development team, to actually support the technical requirements of the program. This would include the program website, SSO, bank APIs, server configuration, and other technical matters.

This is only a cursory overview of the sort of team you'd need to assemble in order to run an incentive program effectively. As you can see, things get both complicated and expensive very quickly. Just imagine what the staffing costs alone for the above scenario would look like for your company, especially if your program is large.

When you go with an outside partner, all these pieces are ready to go on day one. Not only will the above roles be filled, they'll be populated by people with considerable experience with incentive programs. This can save you a massive amount of headache in the long run.

There's one last advantage of working with an outside firm that we should also mention. We're talking about accountability. When you hire a reputable third-party with a proven track record, there's a certain amount of accountability that you know you'll be getting. A good firm will have a system in place for maintaining a proper paper trail, something that allows you to eliminate the potential for internal fraud, theft, money laundering, or any other nefarious activities. You can also rest easy knowing that

203

there are experts handling your program, and that the task of troubleshooting every problem that arises won't consistently fall in your lap.

What to Look for in a Management Partner

So what should you look for in the ideal management partner for your incentive, loyalty or rebate program?

First off, experience is arguably the most important factor. Recall our discussion of what to look for in a bank from Chapter 12. In pointing to a few cautionary tales derived from our own experience, the common theme for bad banks was lack of experience and accountability. The same goes for working with an external firm. If they don't have any experience, they're probably best avoided.

It's important to get specific here. Don't let someone brush off your questions about their previous experience managing incentive programs. How many years have they actually been at this? How many clients have they helped? The higher these numbers, the better. Who are these clients? Were their needs similar to yours? Make sure that you're not jumping on board with a company that's unable to address your organization's specific needs. Do they have references from these clients? They should be comfortable giving you the contact information for the people they've worked with so that you can get firsthand testimonials.

Next, you'll want to spend some time examining the firm itself. How is it structured? Are they based in the United States? One problem that we've seen with some all-in-one incentive management providers is their tendency to outsource as much of their labor as possible to overseas call centers. Many of these management firms simply pay representatives in less developed countries to handle all their customer service needs. This can turn into a big problem, particularly if you have a large program that could require extensive support. If people are unable to access quality customer service, they'll blame it on your brand. Before you know it, your incentive program has created the *opposite* of brand affinity.

Along the same lines, make sure to find out what other services the company offers and how those services are actually delivered. Are they able to answer phone calls, respond to emails, and provide chat support? Unless you plan to train your own dedicated customer service team, this is essential. On top of that, though, can the company provide verification services? Can they plan and book travel for your employee rewards program? You can see how quickly the details begin to pile up. If you're going to work with an outside firm, you want to ensure that you're getting your money's worth. Don't go with a firm that leaves these jobs to you, as these seemingly small administrative tasks can overwhelm you in a hurry.

It's important to be specific when asking these questions, and to hold the firm accountable for providing specific answers. What do we mean by this? Don't simply ask the firm, "Do you handle customer-service calls?" If you do, their response could simply be, "Yes, we take care of customer service." Instead, ask pointed questions about timelines and numbers. "How quickly do you respond to customer-service inquiries? Will our program have a dedicated phone number? What are your operating hours?

Can customers leave a message? What's your response time for email inquiries? What hours will chat support be available?" And of course, "is your call center domestic or overseas?"

Once you start asking these kinds of questions, the difference between a dedicated, in-house customer service team and a foreign call center will quickly make itself obvious. Don't be afraid to nitpick about the details here.

Lastly, it's worth pushing a bit further to see exactly how integrated the firm will be with your own organization. Can they become a literal extension of your own team? Will they be trained to perform the verification and auditing of your reward submissions, or will you still have to do this in-house? And if they will be handling these tasks, can they perform them flawlessly and without error? Find out if they've taken care of these sorts of details for past clients, and then ask those clients about their experience.

One final and very specific note about experience and accountability. Ask your potential partners if they have Errors and Omissions Insurance (E&O) specifically for the purposes of covering incentive programs. From personal experience, we know that these policies can be very difficult to obtain due to the extremely unique nature of these services. For example, unlike the services provided by attorneys or accountants, most insurance carriers simply don't know how to rate and price the coverage required for incentive providers. But assuming the partner has E&O insurance, their potential mistakes (in a worst-case scenario) should be covered, thus limiting your risk.

***

One you've vetted your options, it's time to move forward with the planning process. Before you can get things off the ground, though, there are just a few topics left to cover. As with all things in business, there's one important item which is essential to consider, but which we've yet to address: cost. In the next chapter, we'll discuss some of the costs involved in launching and running an incentive program.

Chapter 16

How Much Do Incentive Programs Cost?

When it comes to pricing out an incentive program, there are essentially two types of costs: marginal costs and service costs. Marginal costs are some of the most obvious, and the easiest to wrap your head around in their entirety. Marginal costs include the following:

- **DEBIT CARDS:** The actual debit cards used in your incentive program, along with their design fees.

- **CARD CARRIERS:** The paper that the debit cards are affixed to, and which includes all of the card's terms and conditions.

- **ENVELOPES:** The mailing envelopes used to distribute the debit cards.

- **POSTAGE AND SHIPPING FEES:** The cost of shipping out debit cards to recipients.

Pretty simple, right? Next up are service fees. This is where things get complicated. Some of these service fees will exist whether your work with an external firm or do things in-house, while others are specific to contracting an outside company. Keep in mind, though, that you don't get to simply avoid those fees by running your program in-house. Instead, they show up on your payroll.

Service costs include:

- **BANK TRANSACTION FEES AND INTERNATIONAL WIRE FEES:** Don't underestimate the cost of bank transaction and international wire fees, as they can add up quickly.

- **WEBSITE DEVELOPMENT, TESTING, AND MAINTENANCE:** Depending on the size and complexity of your incentive program, the cost of developing, testing, and maintaining your web portal can vary widely. We'll discuss this more below in terms of working with an outside firm.

- **WEB HOSTING:** This is an ongoing independent consideration apart from the cost of developing, testing, and maintaining the site.

- **PROJECT MANAGEMENT:** Designing and implementing an incentive program is a complex task, and you'll need dedicated project management to make it work.

- **CUSTOMER SERVICE:** This includes the cost of email support, chat support, and phone support.

- REWARD/SUBMISSION VERIFICATION: For each reward or rebate claim submitted, you have to verify whether the submission is legitimate or not. This verification process becomes a cost center.

- REWARD AUDITING AND REPORT GENERATION: It's essential to stay on top of the numbers as you're launching the program and getting it up and running. You'll also want to periodically check in so that you can measure ROI and make adjustments as needed.

- CLIENT MEETINGS AND DOCUMENT COLLECTION: Working with an outside firm involves meetings and communication, and the firm will likely take this time into account in developing its pricing. Collecting and processing documents will also have to be accounted for.

- CARD AND MERCHANDISE ORDERS: Ordering new cards, ensuring that they've been shipped out, and processing merchandise orders all takes time and resources.

- CARD RELOADS: When cards need to be reloaded, you'll be charged for the service.

- TRAVEL COORDINATION: When employee travel rewards are redeemed, someone has to handle the actual travel booking and coordination process. This comes at a cost.

- PROGRAM ANNOUNCEMENTS, UPDATES, AND NEWSLETTERS: Your program is only effective if participants understand it and are kept up to date. The more engaged your participants are, the more likely they are to take part in the program. You'll need to make regular announcements in the form of email newsletters, and sometimes print mail announcements.

- **TAX AND BANK PROCESSING:** Various accounting and administrative tasks such as 1099 tax processing and bank processing will also become cost centers.

This list isn't meant to be exhaustive, but it gives you a good overview of what you can expect to pay for.

How Incentive Firms Handle Pricing

So, let's assume that you opt to pursue the assistance of an outside firm. Again, this is something we highly recommend. As you're going through the process of evaluating various firms, you might receive cost estimates for launching and running your incentive program.

On the surface, this sounds fairly straightforward. You get a handful of quotes, compare their line item and total costs, and then take those costs into account when determining which incentive firm is the best choice for your organization's need and budget. Right?

In reality, this approach doesn't always go as smoothly as you might think. The reason is simple: Different firms tend to use very different strategies for pricing and billing, which can make comparing two quotes side-by-side a real challenge. Let's look at the two most common ways that an incentive firm will price its services.

The most common pricing approach that you'll encounter involves turning every single cost into an individual line item. Each item is accounted for on its own, leaving little question where your cost centers are going to be. When a firm takes this approach, you'll receive an invoice that looks something like the following:

Invoice #12345

ITEM	QTY	DESCRIPTION	RATE	AMOUNT
Cards	3,256	New Card Orders for March	$9.9	$999
Card Carriers	3,256	Card Carriers for March	$9.9	$999
Envelopes	3,256	Envelopes for March	$9.9	$999
Customer Service	421	Minutes of Customer Service for March	$9.9	$999
Technical	26	Unexpected Technical Fixes March (hours)	$9.9	$999
Reload Fees	1	X% Reload Fees on outstanding cards March	$9.9	$999
Bank Fees	4	Wire Fees for Batch Payment Loads for March	$9.9	$999
Web Hosting	1	Fixed Web Hosting Fee for March	$9.9	$999
Travel Fees	32	Hours for Travel Services in March	$9.9	$999
Travel Costs	1	Total Travel Fees for March Trip Winners	$9.9	$999
Verification	27.5	Submission Verification Hours for March	$9.9	$999
Client Meetings	3	Client Meeting Hours for March	$9.9	$999
Reporting	4.75	Report Hours for March	$9.9	$999
Tax Services	1	Final Costs for Year-End Tax Filing	$9.9	$999
Postage	8,742	First Class Postage for March incl Tax Forms	$9.9	$999
Management	1	Fixed Management Fee for March	$9.9	$999
Total Due				$9,999

As you can see, there are a LOT of different line items here and there could easily be more on some invoices. Most of these fees above are variable, and tied to March's actual volume. However, there are also fixed fees, and unknown fees such as the unexpected technical fixes.

On the one hand, this style of invoicing allows you to confidently assess exactly what you're being billed for across all of your program's cost centers. On the other hand, it's easy to end up feeling a bit like you're being nickeled and dimed. Wire fees? Postage fees down to the penny? If you're running a particularly large program with a lot of line items, making sense of this type of invoice can be both time-consuming and frustrating. It can also make budgeting nearly impossible.

Not every firm takes this approach, though. Another fairly common way to handle invoicing involves charging a fixed monthly fee in addition to a variable service charge based on the total amount of rewards redeemed. For example, a firm may charge a fixed monthly cost of $X in addition to a variable rate of X% of all redeemed incentives per month. This type of invoice will include very few line items. While you may not get to see exactly what each individual program expense costs, this type of invoicing is cleaner, simpler, and a lot easier to plan your budget around.

At this point, you might be wondering what you can expect to pay for an incentive program of a given size. Are we talking a few thousand dollars? Tens of thousands of dollars? What's a reasonable amount, and what's excessive?

We've run a lot of incentive programs over the years, and we've used that experience to put together a cost calculator. You can find our incentive pricing calculator on our website at https://www.level6incentives.com/calculator. Our pricing calculator takes the following variables into account when assembling a cost estimate:

- Where you'll be offering your program (the United States, Canada, or both)

- Type of program you're offering (salesperson incentives, customer loyalty, customer rebates, employee recognition)

- Types of rewards you're including (prepaid single-use branded debit cards, reloadable branded debit cards, virtual debit cards, checks)

- Number of program participants

- Average amount per reward

- Expected total annual dollar amount of reward payouts

- Frequency of reward payouts

- Additional features to be included (custom website, customer service, etc.)

This pricing calculator will give you an instant, ballpark estimate of your costs, which you can use when shopping around for potential program providers. It's not meant to be an exact quote, of course, but it will give you a ballpark number for what you can expect to pay.

Payment Terms for Incentive Companies

Aside from evaluating the costs associated with contracting an outside incentive firm, another important factor you'll want to consider when choosing a firm is the payment terms. What should you expect? What's normal, and what's excessive?

While there's some variability in terms of expectations surrounding the payment schedule for various cost centers, development is one area where you may be asked to fork over a large amount of funds all at once. In fact, some incentive firms will require you to pay for all development work up front. They'll provide you with an initial cost estimate, and you'll have to hand over the entire amount before they get started. Other companies are less demanding and will ask for some kind of a deposit for a portion of development costs (such as 50% of the total amount).

When it comes to pricing out these services, keep in mind that different firms take different approaches. Some firms will use development work as a real profit center, aiming to derive a large portion of total profits from it. Meanwhile, other companies opt to use development as a loss leader. In this scenario, the firm will price their development services as low as possible as a means of engaging and launching a project with a new, hopefully long-term client. Be aware of these various tactics and recognize the various pricing strategies when you see them.

At the end of the day, tactics for both pricing and payment terms can vary widely, as can the total amount you might expect to pay. Ultimately, though, a good incentive provider will generally incorporate both fixed costs and variable costs into their pricing strategy. This allows for predictability on the one hand while still maintaining flexibility according to the program's scope and workflow. Your goal in signing a contract with an incentive firm should be to feel confident that you have a reasonably accurate estimate of what your program's total costs will be, without worrying that you're being overcharged for a level of service that you don't need—or undercharged and short-changed when it comes to the actual program execution and follow-through.

***

At this point, you should have some sense of what it's going to cost to launch your incentive program and keep it running over the long haul. In addition to understanding costs, though, there's one more important thing to consider from a numbers standpoint: The tax implications of your incentive program. In the next chapter, we'll discuss how you should think about taxes when it comes to implementing your incentive program—and when you need to issue tax forms related to the redemption of rewards. We'll also address the question of how to treat points from a tax perspective.

Chapter 17

Taxes and Incentive Programs

So far, we've covered virtually every component related to designing, developing, launching, and running an incentive program. We've talked about how and why incentive programs work, the various kinds of programs you might consider implementing, how to work with a bank, the ins and outs of web portals, the advantages of partnering with an outside firm, and what it costs to run an incentive program.

At this point, you might think that you're ready to launch your first program. But we'd be remiss not to mention one very important (and sometimes boring) consideration: The tax implications of an incentive program.

The realization that your incentive program could create unknown tax implications can hit you like a ton of bricks. Is this a whole can of worms that you're about to open?

How much trouble is this going to be? What is this going to cost you in terms of additional accounting expenses (not to mention overall headache)? Is this whole incentive thing really worth it if you're going to have to deal with a mountain of tax paperwork?

If these and other similar thoughts are running through your head, we don't blame you. But let us assure you, the tax implications of an incentive program don't have to be as complicated or painful as you might think. In this chapter, we're going to look at how incentive rewards are treated from a tax perspective, including how you'll need to account for them when it comes to employees, outside salespeople, and customers. We'll also discuss the question of whether points are actually worth something, and how to account for them when doing your books.

Before we continue, though, we should mention an important disclaimer. This chapter (and, for that matter, this book) is not intended to serve as professional tax or accounting advice. While we're proud of the fact that our firm brings a lot of experience to the table when it comes to incentives, we're not licensed to provide accounting or tax advice. So, at the end of the day, it's important to consult with your accounting and/or tax professional when it comes to specific questions surrounding your individual organization's unique situation.

With that important disclaimer behind us, let's plunge ahead!

Incentives, Rewards, Cash, and Taxes

We're accustomed to thinking of tax liability as something that accompanies cash compensation. If you pay someone for services rendered, that payment has to be accounted for when it comes time to file taxes in the US. Everyone knows this, and it's a pretty straightforward principle. Are you paying someone an hourly wage? You'll need to issue them a W-2 at the end of the year. Did someone perform a one-time contractual service for your company? If so, they'll probably need a 1099-MISC form (we'll discuss 1099-MISC forms in greater detail below). Either way, this is something your organization is (hopefully!) already accustomed to doing.

But what about when it comes to a bonus check? Does that still count as compensation? If so, does it need to be included on an employee's W-2 form? What if instead of a bonus check, you issue them a prepaid reloadable debit card? Does that change the situation? Or, what if instead of paying your employee with cash in one form or another, you compensate them for a job well done with some sort of tangible reward—maybe a vacation, a top-of-the-line flat screen TV, or a gas card? For that matter, what happens if, instead of simply offering these rewards to your employees directly, you reward them with points which can then be exchanged for these and other items?

As it turns out, various bonuses, rewards, and points are accounted for according to specific rules laid out by the IRS in IRS Publication 525, Taxable and Nontaxable Income.[48] Below, we'll look at what IRS Publication 525 has to say about how to account for compensation related to incentive programs, both for employees and external salespeople.

221

Incentive Rewards and Employee Tax Liability

When it comes to your organization's employees, IRS Publication 525 specifically addresses bonuses, awards, and employee achievement award compensation.

According to Publication 525, page 3:

> "Bonuses or awards you receive for outstanding work are included in your income and should be shown on your Form W-2. These include prizes such as vacation trips for meeting sales goals. If the prize or award you receive is goods or services, you must include the fair market value of the goods or services in your income. However, if your employer merely promises to pay you a bonus or award at some future time, it isn't taxable until you receive it, or it is made available to you."

Note that this applies to awards received "for outstanding work." This means that you'll have to account for incentive rewards given to employees if those rewards are the direct result of work that the employee has performed. In these instances, you'll need to include this compensation on the employee's W-2 form. When the compensation takes the form of goods or services rather than actual cash, you'll need to compute the value of those goods or services and add them to the W-2 form.

However, certain employee achievement awards are treated differently. According to Publication 525, page 3:

> "If you receive tangible personal property (other than cash, a gift certificate, or an equivalent

item) as an award for length of service or safety achievement, you generally can exclude its value from your income. However, the amount you can exclude is limited to your employer's cost and can't be more than $1,600 ($400 for awards that aren't qualified plan awards) for all such awards you receive during the year. Your employer can tell you whether your award is a qualified plan award. Your employer must make the award as part of a meaningful presentation, under conditions and circumstances that don't create a significant likelihood of it being disguised pay.

However, the exclusion doesn't apply to the following awards:

A length-of-service award if you received it for less than 5 years of service or if you received another length-of-service award during the year or the previous 4 years.

A safety achievement award if you are a manager, administrator, clerical employee, or other professional employee or if more than 10% of eligible employees previously received safety achievement awards during the year."

As you can see, there's a difference between incentive rewards earned for something like sales performance on the one hand and a small length-of-service gift on the other. The IRS also gives a fairly straightforward and specific example here of how these smaller length-of-service gifts are calculated. If a hypothetical employee receives a total of three length of service gifts—say, a $250 watch, a $1,000 stereo, and a $500 set of golf clubs—that employee is tax liable for those gifts insofar as they exceed the above specified amount of $1,600. In this case, $250 + $1,000 + $500 = $1,750, and $1,750 - $1,600 = $150. So, you would be responsible for accounting for an extra $150 in employee compensation on this employee's W-2 form, and the employee would be responsible for paying taxes on that additional $150.

Incentives and Non-Employees

The above rules are laid out by the IRS with respect to employees who are on your payroll. If you compensate an employee for work performed via the use of an incentive reward, you're expected to include that reward as compensation on the employee's W-2.

But what about non-employees? As we discussed earlier in this book, incentive programs can be especially effective when it comes to changing the behavior of third-party salespeople working for independent dealers—people who aren't on your payroll. If you provide these independent sales reps with incentive rewards, do you have to account for those rewards from a tax perspective? And if so, how do you go about doing it?

If your US-based company has enlisted the services of independent contractors in the past, you're likely already familiar with 1099 forms. If you're not familiar, though, 1099 forms are a series of forms available from the IRS that are used to file an information return in order to account for income not derived from direct employment. The most common 1099 form that you'll likely encounter is the 1099-MISC, which is generally used to account for payments made to independent contractors.

So, let's say you're issuing a reward of some kind to an external salesperson as part of an incentive program you're running in connection with independent dealers. There's one simple question you'll need to ask yourself here: Did this person do some form of work (other than making a purchase, for example, as would be the case with a customer receiving a rebate) in order to achieve the reward in question? If the answer to this question is "yes," then you'll more than likely need to issue that person a 1099 form.

Keep in mind that there's one exception to this rule. A 1099-MISC form only has to be filed if the third-party salesperson in question received a total of $600 USD or more in a given calendar year. So, if your incentive reward program involves issuing small rewards to a large number of salespeople, you're less likely to end up in a scenario where you're having to file a large number of 1099 forms. (Companies outside of the US should consult their tax professional on the rules for non-employee reward taxation.)

It's not uncommon to run into people in the incentive industry who will tell you that this isn't important or isn't something to worry about. But we're here to tell you, this isn't something you can ignore. The law is the law. And if you're running a large incentive program that involves thousands upon thousands of dollars in payments, failing to properly account for all of those expenses (and for all of the income associated with them for the people receiving them) may cause you major problems down the road.

When it comes to adding reward totals as compensation to employee W-2 forms, your accounting department or external accountant will likely be able to handle this without a lot of extra hassle. But when you're dealing with external sales reps, things are a bit more complicated. You'll need to collect the Social Security number of each person in order to issue them a 1099, and it's obviously important to treat this data with care. One of the easiest ways to handle this is with a secure online form that's built into your web portal, accompanied by the proper opt-in language to ensure that the recipient in question understands what data they're providing to you and why. This form can essentially serve as a virtual W-9 form and even include the requisite language from the W-9. (Some CPA's believe a paper W-9 is required, although we don't personally subscribe to this belief, given that paper forms are far less secure than digitally protected forms).

In our experience, it's generally best to let the outside incentive firm you're working with handle the entire 1099 process. This is especially true if you're dealing with a massive number of 1099s. Of course, if you work in a field such as accounting and already have a ton of experience dealing with something like this, then that may change your situation somewhat. But for the most part, we've found that it's typically easier for companies to simply outsource this work to their incentive partner.

While you may not be handling the filing of 1099s on your own, it's worth pointing out that the 1099-MISC form actually includes two separate boxes where compensation can be accounted for: Box 3, "Other Income," and Box 7, "Nonemployee Compensation." According to the IRS's Instructions for Form 1099-MISC, the difference in these seemingly similar boxes is that Box 3 is for prizes and awards unrelated to services performed, whereas Box 7 would include compensation in exchange for the performance of actual services. Typically, we recommend putting the value from winning random drawings in Box 3, and anything else explicitly earned goes into Box 7. The advantage to Box 3 is a slightly lower tax burden for most filers. Keep this in mind if attempting to fill out a 1099 on your own.

Additionally, you'll need to file something with the IRS known as a 1096 form. This serves as kind of master informational tax form. It's used to summarize all of the 1099s that you're issuing to other individuals. In other words, the 1096 form won't be sent to any reward recipients or third-party salespeople—it's only sent to the IRS for informational purposes. Typically, a copy of the 1096 is sent to our partners' payroll and/or tax departments so they have an official record.

Are Points Worth Something?

At this point, we've looked at how to account for rewards issued to employees and non-employees. By accounting for incentive rewards properly, you'll ensure that you're in compliance with tax law and IRS requirements.

There's one more issue to tackle here, though—the notion of points.

Maybe the thought hadn't occurred to you up until now but take a moment to ask yourself what points are exactly. How should you handle them? If you're issuing points to your employees that can be exchanged for merchandise or prepaid debit cards, do those points then count as a form of cash compensation? And if so, how do you account for them?

Believe it or not, the IRS actually specifically addresses the issue of "prize points" in Publication 525. On page 32 of Publication 525, the IRS outlines exactly how points should be accounted for:

> "If you are a salesperson and receive prize points redeemable for merchandise that are awarded by a distributor or manufacturer to employees of dealers, you must include their fair market value in your income. The prize points are taxable in the year they are paid or made available to you, rather than in the year you redeem them for merchandise."

In other words, points do indeed count as a form of compensation, and they do have to be included as income when tax time rolls around.

We'll be honest with you here: We've seen 99% of companies choose to ignore this rule. But that doesn't mean that ignoring it is the right thing (or the legal thing) to do. Technically speaking, points should be included in your accounting. They're on the books. And the IRS expects them to be accounted for from a tax perspective, too.

Now, if the prize points are redeemed for something in a given calendar year, then you'll simply follow the guidelines provided above as they relate to the inclusion of the fair market value of various prizes, travel awards, and so on. But what if someone doesn't use all of their points in a given year? That's when they become taxable in and of themselves. The fair market value of the points themselves will then need to be accounted for.

Assuming you and your tax advisors have a risk-adverse viewpoint surrounding this rule, and you want to follow it to the letter of the law, what's the best way to handle this from a practical perspective? To simplify things as much as possible, we advise our clients to do something that we call a "year-end cash out" of points. Essentially, this is where you automatically disperse the value of any accumulated points on a given date at the end of the year. It can be a good idea to notify program participants that their points will be cashed out automatically if they're not redeemed, and to encourage them to go ahead and redeem their points before that happens. If the deadline rolls around and someone has leftover points, though, you simply load a prepaid debit card with the corresponding cash value of the points and issue it to the recipient in question. This keeps you in compliance with the requirements laid out by the IRS and ensures that things add up from an accounting perspective at the end of the year. And it's far kinder than taxing a third-party rep on the value of abstract points.

Rebates and Taxes

What about customer rebates? What are the tax considerations with those? Here's some good news, and we'll keep it simple. The IRS doesn't require any tax reporting for the purposes of issuing customer rebates. So rest easy.

Incentive Rewards and Our Own Taxes

How does running an incentive program affect your own tax liability as a company? Well, it's generally possible to write off the various costs associated with running an incentive program as a business expense. This doesn't just include the fees paid out to an external firm, the cost of setting up and maintaining a web portal, and so on. In addition, this means that you ought to be able to deduct the costs associated with issuing the reward funding itself. In other words, these tax liable rewards that you're issuing to others can be deducted from your annual gross revenue in determining your company's own tax liability. As we mentioned in an earlier chapter, incentive programs are often expensed as a marketing cost; however, it's worth giving some consideration to how you want to treat rewards from a cost center perspective.

***

To wrap up, there's something we said at the beginning of this chapter which bears repeating here. We're not tax experts or accountants, and we don't claim to have all of the answers when it comes to your particular organization's unique scenario and needs. We highly recommend that you contact an accountant or tax professional when it comes to ensuring that you're properly accounting for your incentive program.

***

So, that's it! From an accounting perspective, we've addressed a lot of major questions here. But there's one last practicality to consider when it comes to working with third-party dealers. When you go to actually issue the payment of rewards to external salespeople, do you issue those rewards to each individual salesperson directly? Or, do you pay out those incentives to the franchise owner or dealer principal, allowing them to then distribute the rewards on their own? As it turns out, the answer to this question can have a major impact on the success (or failure) of your incentive program. We'll address that in the next chapter.

Chapter 18

Paying Out Third-party Rewards

We've covered a lot of ground so far, and we know you're probably itching to develop and launch your first program. But before we wrap up with some final thoughts on rolling out your program and best practices, there's one last detail we need to discuss.

As we've mentioned previously, one of the most effective types of incentive programs that we've seen involves working with channel partners such as third-party dealers and distributors. Why? Well, influencing the behavior of independent sales representatives with traditional means tends to present all sorts of difficulties. They're not your employees, and you're not cutting their paychecks. Why should they listen to you? What reason would they have to steer potential customers toward your product rather than your competitor's?

That's where incentive rewards come in. With the right incentive program in place, we've seen companies liquidate inventory, grow sales by more than 20% per year, and more. A well-designed and properly implemented incentive program has the power to outperform virtually every other form of marketing or sales strategy out there.

But, there's one major thing that you'll need to address when it comes to incentivizing these independent sales reps. How do you actually issue their rewards?

That may sound like a strange question, but it's actually of paramount importance that you consider it now. There are essentially two options here. On the one hand, you can just issue incentives to business owners or dealer principals and allow them to further distribute the rewards to employees individually. Alternatively, you can issue the rewards directly to each of the third-party salespeople on your own. Both approaches come with their own advantages and disadvantages. Let's take a look at each of them in turn.

Paying Incentives to Business Owners or Dealer Principals

Your first option involves issuing rewards directly to the owner of the business, or to the dealer principal in charge of a number of individual locations.

The advantage here is primarily logistical. Rather than having to deal with dozens (or thousands) of individual sales reps on your own, you can simply issue rewards to the person in charge of supervising those individual salespeople. This can cut down on some hassle on your end, as it means that you can likely reduce the number of individual customer support inquiries you receive. You may also be able to simplify the amount of paperwork that you have to process, although that depends on the bookkeeping practices of the dealer in question and how helpful they are when it comes to coordinating.

While this may sound attractive, there's a major disadvantage that can spell disaster for your whole incentive program. Simply put, what happens if the people in charge never actually distribute those rewards to their employees?

This isn't purely a question of conscience. Sure, it's possible that the dealer principal or business owner might opt to keep the rewards for themselves. But it doesn't have to be as nefarious as that. People are busy, and there's a chance that the business owner in question might forget to distribute the rewards in question. Or, maybe they'll make a mistake and fail to issue some of them. Maybe an employee will only get a fraction of what they were owed.

The specifics aren't that important here. More relevant for our purposes is the end result, which is ultimately the same in every case. At the end of the day, paying out incentive rewards to a dealer principal or business owner could potentially result in independent salespeople failing to receive them. And if that happens, the effectiveness of your incentive program is going to be severely limited.

Issuing Rewards Directly to Salespeople

Rather than running the risk outlined above, a much safer option is to issue rewards directly to the salespeople who have earned them. When you do this, you completely bypass the dealer principal or business owner. That means that there's no risk of the salespeople missing out on the rewards they deserve.

The only real disadvantage to this approach is the added logistical complications that are involved. As outlined in the previous chapter on incentives and taxes, you'll likely have to issue 1099-MISC forms to independent salespeople when they earn rewards. This involves the collection, processing, and storage of a lot of data, not to mention a ton of extra paperwork. If you're working with a good incentive provider, that shouldn't be a problem. If you're trying to handle everything on your own, though, it's worth considering the extra work that will come along with taking this approach.

On the flip side, the advantage of paying out incentives directly to salespeople actually goes beyond simply guaranteeing that they receive their rewards. Consider the fact that by issuing rewards to dealer principals or business owners, you're potentially missing out on the opportunity to create brand affinity in the salesperson recipient. If they're getting their reward from their employer, there's a good chance that they'll simply associate all of the positive things about that reward with their employer rather than with your company. When you issue rewards directly to salespeople, though, they make the connection right away between the reward and your brand. And considering that they're on the front line, dealing directly with customers each and every day, creating brand affinity with independent salespeople is extremely valuable to your long-term sales goals.

Recipient Conflict

Let's assume that you attempt to pay salespeople cash rewards directly, as described above. Unfortunately, you may occasionally face backlash from some of the business owners at your channel partners. Why? Well, they may look at your incentive program as a means to interfering with their standard compensation plan. If you're incentivizing their salespeople, you're swaying their behavior (by design) and impacting the products they sell. It's possible your program may interfere with an owner's goals. You're also allowing them to earn more money, which strangely enough can offend certain business owners.

When and if this backlash occurs, we normally recommend the following methods to overcome these objections. First, explain calmly that your incentive program is 100% optional. Nobody is forcing anybody to participate. (Your opt-in forms should clearly state the optional nature of the program as well). If this doesn't work, and the backlash becomes more widespread, create a one-time dealership opt-in form for each location. This includes a physical or digital signature of the business owner, and affirms their approval for their reps to participate. The communication also should reiterate that these funds will not be dispersed in any other fashion, no discounts, rebates to the dealer, etc. From experience, even when business owners occasionally object, they'll ultimately relent and allow their team to participate, especially when it's clearly stated that the funds aren't available in any alternative forms.

***

With this last detail accounted for, it's time to think about launching your first incentive program. In the next chapter, we'll touch on some of the most important things you'll need to consider when it comes time for rollout.

Chapter 19

Program Launch
& Rollout

You've made it! Congratulations! Understanding what incentives are, how they work, and how to design and launch your own program is no simple task. We've covered a lot of detail in this book, and you've nearly made it to the end. It's time to take action. You're officially ready to launch your first incentive program.

Now we want to address exactly how you can go about launching your program, along with what the rollout process is and what it ought to look like. The most common type of incentive program that we assist clients with is one that's targeted at independent dealers and sales reps, and that's the type of program rollout that we'll examine in greater detail here. We'll look at a few different examples of how you might approach launching your program, with the relative advantages and disadvantages of each. Even if your program is internally focused, many of these same principles should still apply.

Launching a Program with Independent Dealers

Let's assume that your company is a preferred brand of some kind that works with independent dealers for sales and distribution. You've decided to develop an incentive program targeted at these independent salespeople, with the goal of encouraging them to push your products harder than those offered by your competitors.

When it comes to launching your program, one of your biggest considerations has to be the process of actually reaching these salespeople. How will you let them know that your program exists? If these sales reps aren't aware of what your program is, how it works, and what it can offer them in terms of rewards, you'll be unlikely to see much in the way of results. The better educated these independent salespeople are about your incentive program, the better.

If you currently have some sort of CRM or Learning Management System in place for your products, there's a chance that you might already have the email addresses for these independent sales reps. If so, that's great news for you. Why? Because a highly effective way to roll out your program involves the use of an email marketing campaign.

You might already engage in quite a bit of email marketing, in which case the efficacy of a good email campaign is something you'll be familiar with. If you're new to email marketing, though, you may want to work with your incentive firm or a third-party marketer to set up a drip campaign. Drip email campaigns deliver a series of messages to recipients over time and can be a highly affordable way to raise awareness with respect to your new incentive program. Aside from how easy it can be to set up a drip campaign, one of the other major advantages of email marketing is how affordable it is. Some services are free, and those that aren't tend to cost a fraction of other forms of communication or advertising.

Of course, all of this assumes that you already have the email addresses of these independent salespeople. If you don't, then an email marketing campaign obviously won't be an option. And in our experience, it's not a typical scenario for companies to have access to email addresses for the sales reps associated with all their channel partners.

Fortunately, though, there are other strategies available to you if email marketing isn't an option. In fact, our go-to recommendation for the launch and rollout for a new incentive program is direct mail.

Wait, direct mail? Seriously? Yes, we mean it. We know, we know—direct mail is old school. And compared to something like email marketing, it can be expensive. But if done right, direct mail can be extremely effective. You'll be putting your brand directly in front of salespeople in a way that other forms of communication aren't capable of accomplishing. As with email marketing, we recommend taking a drip campaign approach to direct mail. Sending out a series of mailers over the course of several weeks is generally much more effective than a single envelope.

Aside from email and direct mail, another highly effective strategy for launching a new incentive program involves working with your field sales reps. They're going to be visiting your dealers anyway, and this is a perfect opportunity to promote your program launch. Your field sales reps can talk to dealers and independent salespeople individually, educating them about your new incentive program in a memorable way. Your field reps can also drop off promotional materials, which will help to keep your program (and your brand) top-of-mind.

As the saying goes, you only get one chance to make a first impression. It's essential that you lead with your best possible reward offer. You want these independent sales reps to be excited by the earning and reward potential associated with your brand. Remember what motivates salespeople and play to those desires. Of course, making a good first impression isn't restricted to the content of your reward program, but also the form of presentation. Make sure that your website is free of errors, and that the user experience is as simple and straightforward as possible. The better the user experience, the more likely program participants will actually engage with your program.

**

That's it! You're ready to launch your first incentive program. In the next and final chapter, we'll offer some closing advice in the form of best practices. These strategies will help you ensure that your first ever program is a resounding success.

Chapter 20

Incentive Program
Best Practices

A lmost there... You've made it to the final chapter. At this point, you've learned all the basics that you need to know in order to properly conceptualize, design, and launch a highly effective incentive program.

In this book, we've covered:

- What incentives are

- The concept of behavior modification

- Incentive rewards vs. employee recognition

- ROI of incentive programs

- Training and orientation

- Incentives for independent sales reps, employees, and customers

- Customer loyalty programs

- Incentive delivery mechanisms including prepaid debit cards, reloadable debit cards, virtual debit cards, and merchandise & travel

- What to look for (and what to avoid) in a bank

- Designing an incentive program

- The ins and outs of web portals

- Working with an outside management partner

- The cost of incentive programs

- Incentive tax implications

- Issuing incentive payments to independent salespeople

- Successfully launching a program

That's a lot of information, and you deserve a pat on the back for absorbing all of it. But before we wrap up, we want to take the time to offer some closing tips and best practices when it comes to running a successful incentive program.

While not exhaustive, the following best practices are things that we've found to be important across the board for our clients over the years. Whether your company is large or small—and regardless of what industry you're in—the following tips should be helpful in maximizing the potential ROI of your incentive program.

Ready? Let's take a look.

Be Consistent, but Keep Things Fresh

We know, we know—that's contradictory advice. But hear us out on this one.

On the one hand, consistency is a key factor in determining the success of your incentive program. If you communicate your rewards clearly and keep your program consistent, you'll have a much better chance of reaching your goals than if your program is perceived as inconsistent or poorly put together.

What does this look like in practice? One area we see incentive programs falter is the delivery of rewards. When a program first launches, reward recipients might receive their incentive within a couple of weeks. But a year into the program, things have begun to unravel. Now, when an employee or independent sale rep submits a request for a reward, it takes two months for them to receive it due to corporate complacency. In the meantime, they end up calling customer service or sending a frustrated email asking why they haven't received their reward yet. This literally creates the opposite of brand affinity, as it creates more work for the person in question and also gives them the impression that your organization doesn't have it together.

We've also seen companies institute massive rule and program overhauls in a way that alienates program participants. It's normal to make small changes to incentives and rules as you go, but completely rebuilding a program from the ground up tends to present some major challenges in terms of retention and program participation. This is one reason to ensure that you go to the trouble of thoroughly designing your program and laying everything out ahead of time. The more work you put into planning things prior to launch, the less likely it is that you'll need to overhaul your program later.

All of this being said, remember that staying consistent doesn't imply being monotonous. It's a good idea to keep things fresh. If you're using a web portal, you can add new merchandise and travel options on an annual, quarterly, or even monthly basis. These sorts of changes can be a good thing, as they give you a reason to remind program participants of the rewards available to them.

Take the Stairs

If you're the sort of person who's trying to stay in shape and work in 10,000 steps per day, you've likely heard that it's a good idea to take the stairs. We're giving you the same advice here. Well, sort of.

All joking aside, we recommend implementing a stair-step approach to your incentive program. What does this mean? Essentially, a stair-step approach implies that the higher a program participant's sales numbers go, the more they'll be able to earn in terms of rewards. This isn't just linear, though. We're not simply saying that more sales should equal more rewards. Instead, higher tiers of sales should correspond to higher tiers of rewards.

For example, say that a salesperson manages to sell 10 products in a year. If so, they're entitled to $100 in rewards. But for the next 10 products that they sell in that same year, they receive $150 in rewards. And if they manage to sell an additional 10 products, they'll get $200 in rewards for that final ten. This can continue on to whatever degree seems reasonable based on your goals, budget, and organization.

The implications of this are huge, and we've seen it work incredibly well for our clients. With a linear 1:1 reward program, there's less and less incentive for a salesperson to sell more once they've reached a certain threshold. They've worked hard, they've gotten their rewards, and the fact that the year is coming to a close does nothing to motivate them to work harder. With a stair step reward program, though, the opposite is true. The more they sell, the greater their incentive to break through to the next reward level. This can be extremely effective toward the end of the year, when salespeople will push themselves to reach the highest reward level possible before things reset on January 1st.

This tactic isn't just highly effective. It's also easier to implement than you might think. With an online reward portal, all of this can be automated. You won't have to worry about manually calculating these sorts of rewards for each and every employee, which makes this strategy even more viable.

Spin & Win

Gamification is a great way to get people excited about something. People like to have fun and turning something into a game is a great way to make it fun. Not all audiences and demographics respond well to gamification, of course, so it's important to know your program participants and act accordingly.

Setting up random rewards in a "spin & win" format can create major excitement and anticipation—especially if there's large variance in reward amounts. For example, the average reward could be something like $100, but amounts could vary from as low as $25 to as much as $10,000. If hitting a certain sales threshold allows your program participants the opportunity to potentially earn that $10,000 bonus, you'll find that some of them will work harder for that chance than for a guaranteed (but significantly lower) amount.

Keep It Simple

Throughout this book, we've laid out a lot of different strategies for setting up incentive programs. But while there are certainly plenty of varying approaches that you might take to setting up and running a program—much of which is determined by the needs of your organization and the type of audience you're targeting—we can safely say that all of these programs should have one thing in common. They need to be simple to understand and participate in.

This may sound like obvious advice, but you have to remember that your program participants are busy people with a million different things floating around in their minds. If your program's website is confusing, or if the rules seem complicated, they're simply going to ignore it. If you send out an email that's thousands of words long and asks them to jump through a dozen hoops in order to get their rewards, they're probably not going to participate in your program.

The easier it is for participants to take part in your incentive program, the better. Similarly, the more automation there is on your end, the less work there will be, and the less room for error in the long run. Automation is your friend and using a web portal is a great way to automate things.

Communication is Key

As you'll recall from the second chapter of this book, the purpose of an incentive program is to modify the behavior of your target audience. But in order to modify the behavior of your employees (or customers, or independent sales reps), your target audience needs to know what your program is, what's being offered, how to participate, and when they'll receive their rewards. And they can't know these things if you don't communicate them.

This may sound like an obvious statement, but we've seen companies running incentive programs where communication was an afterthought at best. Program participants were confused about how the rewards on offer actually worked, and some people had the impression that the program was derelict or defunct. By communicating regularly with your target audience, you're keeping your incentive program top-of-mind and ensuring that they stay motivated to participate.

We've found that monthly is a good frequency for sending out notifications and updates, although quarterly might be an option in some cases. There's one caveat here, though. More communication isn't always better. At some point, the law of diminishing returns starts to apply. And beyond a certain threshold, you'll likely find that your email open rates decline significantly. Sending out emails every single day, for example, is unnecessary for making announcements relevant to your incentive program. They'll be packed with filler, and people will ignore them. Then, when it comes time to make an important announcement—such as something related to new merchandise on your web portal, or new rules for the program—you'll find that most recipients fail to open the email.

Simply put, communicate clearly, concisely, and regularly—but not so frequently that your program participants start to tune you out. Keep an eye on your email open rates and adjust your frequency accordingly.

Make It Worth Their While

As we discussed in an earlier chapter, different employees are motivated by different things. Some employees just have a solid work ethic, while others work harder as a result of positive feedback and customer interaction.

People in sales, meanwhile, tend to be driven primarily by earning potential. Sure, salespeople are motivated by other factors, too. But at the end of the day, sales is a tough and exhausting job. People don't do it just because they love interacting with customers, or because they like to travel (as many regional sales reps are required to do). They do it because their potential for earnings is virtually unlimited.

With that in mind, an effective incentive program targeted at salespeople has to be perceived as worth their while in order to be effective. If the rewards aren't commensurate in their minds with the amount of time and energy that they'll have to expend to achieve a specific sales goal (and to participate in the program), then they'll be unlikely to take part.

Much of this has to do with the value of your rewards in comparison to the value of the items being sold, along with the amount of time involved in closing a sale. For example, offering a $10 reward per sale to a sales rep at a car dealership with the aim of incentivizing them to sell more of your company's luxury car model isn't going to work. This may sound obvious, but we've seen some grossly mismatched incentive programs over the years.

The opposite of this is true, too, of course. It's certainly possible to over-reward program participants. By spending too much on rewards relative to the total revenue generated will simply cut into your return on investment.

The key here, then, is balance. Your goal is to find the sweet spot. You want a reward amount that creates optimal levels of motivation and participation on the one hand, while simultaneously maximizing your ROI on the other. If you can find that balance, the likelihood of your program being successful increases exponentially.

Remember the Incentives vs. Recognition Distinction

In Chapter 3, we considered the differences between *incentive rewards* on the one hand and *recognition awards* on the other. It's important to keep this distinction in mind when designing your program. So let's review.

Incentives are used to modify behavior. In this sense, they're almost always forward-looking. You're setting clearly defined goals that you want your employees to hit and rewarding them once they hit those goals.

Employee recognition awards, on the other hand, are more backward-looking. More often than not, recognition awards aren't something that employees are actively working to achieve. Maybe the details of such an award aren't even announced in advance, and receiving the award is a surprise for the employees involved.

Even when recognition awards are forward-looking in the form of an announced competition, they're still different from incentives. Where incentives are made available to everyone, recognition awards are by definition limited to a specific number of employees. Think of it this way: While an incentive reward might involve paying out a specific dollar amount in the form of a prepaid debit card to any employee who crosses a specific sales threshold, a recognition award might be given to the top 3 salespeople at your company.

What are the consequences of this? Incentive rewards motivate your whole team. Everyone stands a chance (in theory, at least) of receiving the incentive, and the performances of other people in the organization has nothing to do with their ability to receive the reward in question.

With recognition awards, though, things are different. When the award is first announced—say at the beginning of a quarter—everyone has an equal chance of winning the award. But toward the end of the quarter, only the top handful of salespeople will remain in the running to win. Maybe your top six or seven salespeople all stand a legitimate chance of ending up in spots one through three at the end of the quarter. Meanwhile, the other 20 or 30 salespeople on your team are way too far behind. So, what happens? While the handful of people at the top will all work extra hard to either pull ahead or maintain their lead, the rest of your team doesn't receive any extra motivation. They're totally out of the running anyway, which means they have no reason to work harder at the end of the quarter.

So, what's the takeaway here? At the end of the day, incentive rewards and recognition awards both have their advantages and disadvantages. That's why it's so effective to use them in combination, and we recommend doing so whenever possible. But regardless of which type of program you're launching (or if you're launching both at the same time), the important thing is to be clear on the differences. That way, you'll be able to clearly communicate the nature of your program to its potential participants.

Focus on Your Goals

We've talked throughout this book about the different ways you can design, implement, and run a successful incentive, rebate, or loyalty program. Want to boost customer satisfaction? Incentivize your customer support team. Need to increase sales of a particular product via third-party dealers? Create an incentive program for independent salespeople. Looking to reward your customers without using discounts and coupons? Offer them a product rebate.

Whatever it is you're looking to accomplish—be it higher sales, happier customers, or whatever else—incentive programs are highly effective tools. But in order for them to work, you have to be clear on what your goals are.

You'd be surprised at how often we've seen incentive programs in place without any clear goal in mind. Companies will regularly launch incentive programs without a solid sense of what they're trying to accomplish, and this leads to an inability to really measure ROI. It's not enough to simply say that you want to increase sales, either. In order to help you design the right program, your incentives partner should challenge you for answers to questions that ferret out the real goal of the project. How *much* do you want to increase sales? What are you spending on the incentive program? What does success look like to you? What sort of opportunity cost is involved in launching and running the program? Meaningful answers to these questions are goal-dependent. The clearer your goals are from the beginning, the easier it will be to measure success every step of the way.

We should also stress here that understanding goals isn't simply a matter of laying out numbers in a spreadsheet. Remember that the ultimate objective of any incentive program isn't simply the achievement of certain sales numbers or customer service feedback scores. Rather, the objective is behavior modification. Whether we're talking about employees, independent salespeople, or customers, you're not just trying to reach certain benchmarks—you're trying to modify the ongoing behavior of individual people.

Keeping this reality in mind is essential if you want to actually do things like increase sales or customer lifetime value, because it's human behavior modification that's going to result in the ROI you're looking for. This means that your incentive program has to actually speak to the people you're looking to motivate, whether it's a sales team, a customer support team, your customers, or someone else. If you're conscious of what's going to motivate a particular audience, you're much more likely to design an incentive program that delivers the results you're looking for.

Do Your Homework

In one sense, incentive programs are quite simple. You're looking to modify specific behaviors in order to achieve certain goals, and the necessary reward mechanisms don't have to be complicated.

At the same time, though, an effective program can be quite complex. There are a ton of moving pieces involved. If you don't invest enough time up front in planning your program ahead of time, it's highly unlikely that you'll reach the goals you set out to achieve.

With this in mind, it's important to do your homework before jumping in and launching an incentive program. First, you'll want to identify the key players involved in your program. This can include independent salespeople, department heads, employees, managers, administrators, and anyone else with a role to play. Next, you'll want to define your goals as discussed above. From there, you've got to set reasonable expectations for your program. And lastly, it's essential that you create a detailed timeline leading up to program launch.

All of this requires a lot of time and dedication. An incentive program isn't something you can pull together overnight. By giving yourself time and space to do your homework, you'll be setting yourself up for success.

Don't Overlook Security

Unless you're an IT security specialist, you're probably not an expert when it comes to data security. Starting at the top, let's define the most important aspect to remember: The safety and security of your participants' personal data must be your #1 priority. If personal data is breached, you and your organization could be in serious trouble. But don't fear, there are a few common safeguards to remember. That said, we're not going to cover everything about program security here, but we want to highlight a few important aspects to consider.

First, make sure that your server is running a modern operating system, and is managed by a proven third party with demonstrated success in network security. This server should come bundled with common sense security features such as a firewall and virus scanning. The web portal itself should be running modern code with common safeguards against hacks, code injections and other attacks.

Second, consider the data that you want to encrypt on the database. At a minimum, you'll want to encrypt your participants' Social Security numbers and passwords. You'll likely want to consider encrypting their home addresses and phone numbers as well. This is the most sensitive information. What does encrypting mean? It means that even if your server were breached somehow, the offending party would have almost zero chance of decrypting (read: understanding) the encrypted data. In fact, encrypted data should also mean that program management also won't be able to see this information without an advanced developer and a security key involved.

Finally, don't forget the security of offline data as it's equally important. In fact, in recent years, it's become more common for our clients to prefer a purely online, server-based information flow. What does this mean? It means that reports aren't downloaded or emailed to individual workstations, they're simply accessed securely online. Payment files are handled securely with SSL APIs rather than downloading and re-uploading. This advice might sound somewhat counterintuitive, but the rationale is this: Most servers are more secure today than individual workstations. And considering how many workstations are now portable (laptops and tablets), the entire machine could be stolen and all of the data would be exposed.

This is a *very* high-level overview of security. Typically these incentive programs aren't major targets for attacks, but you'll want to just be mindful that your IT team and your management partner are paying attention to security.

Be Careful When Choosing a Bank

As we discussed in Chapter 12, finding a bank that's willing to work with you on an incentive program can be a challenge. Most banks don't offer the sorts of services you need. For this reason, it can be tempting to jump on board with the first bank you find that's reasonably priced and ready to move forward with your program.

But as we mentioned in that same chapter, this would be a huge mistake. We learned the hard way that there are some seriously questionable "banking partners" out there. That's why it's essential to check references and ask tough questions before entering into any sort of an agreement. If you get a bad feeling from a bank, there's probably a good reason why. Trust your intuition here. And if you get a bad reference from one of the bank's past clients, it's better to walk away and look elsewhere.

Ultimately, you want to find a banking partner with lots of incentive experience and strong references. If you can find a bank that fits the bill from the very beginning, you'll save yourself a lot of potential headache down the road. Remember, it is your brand that will bear the burden of any misfortune.

Work with a Management Partner

Back in Chapter 15, we talked about the advantages of working with an outside firm to design and implement your incentive program. While this isn't absolutely essential, we highly recommend it—especially if this is your first attempt at creating a program.

Why work with a management partner? There are a few reasons. First, as we mentioned above, incentive programs are complex. There's a steep learning curve involved. If you've never run a program on your own, going from zero knowledge to successfully implementing your first program is going to be challenging.

Secondly, an outside firm can save you quite a bit of money. While you might be tempted to run a program on your own under the assumption that you'll be able to cut costs, this is rarely what ends up happening. You think you'll save money by keeping things in house, sure. But in reality, the number of unanticipated expenses quickly grows... and before you know it, you're spending much more than if you'd simply gone with an outside firm to begin with. Remember that a dedicated incentive firm will have practices and efficiencies in place ahead of time that can translate to cost savings. Plus, they won't be making the sort of costly first-timer mistakes that you'll be prone to making.

Lastly, there are a ton of roles involved in running an incentive program. You've got to think about sales, creative, administration, customer service, financials, and more. Do you really have the staff to dedicate to these tasks? Can you afford to distract your existing team members with these added responsibilities? If the answer isn't a resounding "yes," then an external firm is probably the better choice.

***

In this book, we've covered everything you need to know about incentive programs. We've talked about what they are, how they work, why they're effective, and how to implement them. After many years in the incentive business, we can confidently say that incentive programs are capable of producing better ROI than just about any other form of marketing or sales strategy. Simply put, incentives are hard to beat.

Now it's your turn. It's time to design and launch your own incentive program. We wish you the best, and we're excited about your future successes. Good luck!

Endnotes

1   https://www.nber.org/digest/nov03/w9727.html

2   https://www.wilsongroup.com/wp-content/uploads/2011/03/Innovation-Incentives.pdf

3   https://www.medicalnewstoday.com/articles/321037.php

4   https://www.investopedia.com/terms/r/rational-choice-theory.asp

5   https://www.economist.com/news/2009/03/20/herbert-simon

6   https://www.ncbi.nlm.nih.gov/pubmed/17835457

7   https://www.behavioraleconomics.com/resources/books/thinking-fast-and-slow-daniel-kahneman/

8   https://www.nytimes.com/2008/08/24/books/review/Friedman-t.html

9   https://www.forbes.com/sites/digitalrules/2009/12/17/its-the-incentives-stupid/#716a5da33904

10   http://freakonomics.com/2013/10/23/what-makes-people-do-what-they-do/

11   https://ianayres.yale.edu/

12   http://nobel.zufe.edu.cn/uploads/1/file/public/201712/20171207185435_1sfueu8i2x.pdf

13   https://news.gallup.com/opinion/gallup/205670/steps-creating-engagement-every-day.aspx

14   https://www.forbes.com/sites/georgebradt/2017/11/15/the-abcs-of-changing-undesirable-behavior-habits/#7f89aaa9106f

15   https://www.researchgate.net/publication/48926209_Labor_Supply_of_New_York_City_Cabdrivers_One_Day_at_a_Time

16   https://hbr.org/2007/07/the-making-of-an-expert

17   https://techcrunch.com/2016/12/19/79-percent-of-americans-now-shop-online-but-its-cost-more-than-convenience-that-sways-them/

18   https://ianayres.yale.edu/

19   https://www.webfx.com/blog/business-advice/the-cost-of-advertising-nationally-broken-down-by-medium/

20   https://blog.wishpond.com/post/78017573553/21-random-stats-and-facts-about-google-adwords

21   https://www.wordstream.com/blog/ws/2015/05/21/how-much-does-ad-words-cost

22   https://optinmonster.com/email-marketing-vs-social-media-perfor-mance-2016-2019-statistics/

23   https://www.templafy.com/blog/how-many-emails-are-sent-every-day-top-email-statistics-your-business-needs-to-know/

24   https://www.huffpost.com/entry/what-science-says-about-dis-counts_b_8511224?guccounter=1

25   https://www.mediapost.com/appyawards/

26   https://www.canadianbusiness.com/innovation/how-to-avoid-the-pricing-race-to-the-bottom/

27   https://www.emeraldinsight.com/doi/abs/10.1108/EJM-11-2014-0725

28   https://www.shiftelearning.com/blog/statistics-on-corporate-training-and-what-they-mean-for-your-companys-future

29   https://www.mdx.ac.uk/courses/professional-prac-tice-and-work-based-learning

30   https://businesstrainingexperts.com/knowledge-center/training-roi/profit-ing-from-learning/

31   https://www.shiftelearning.com/blog/statistics-value-of-employee-train-ing-and-development

32   https://www.actuary.org/content/drivers-2017-health-insurance-premi-um-changes-0

33   https://www.entrepreneur.com/article/281511

34   https://www.rand.org/content/dam/rand/pubs/research_reports/RR200/RR254/RAND_RR254.sum.pdf

35   https://www.classy.org/blog/study-says-add-a-charitable-incentive-at-work-to-boost-productivity/

36   https://hbr.org/2014/10/the-value-of-keeping-the-right-customers

37   https://www.freshstep.com/paw-points/

38   https://www.dmnews.com/customer-experience/news/13055096/6-per-sonalization-practices-from-walgreens-balance-rewards-program

39   https://www.dmnews.com/channel-marketing/multi-omnichannel/news/13059512/walgreens-loyalty-program-debut-intensifies-drug-store-loyalty-battle

40   https://www.forbes.com/sites/shephyken/2017/03/25/the-best-loyalty-programs-go-beyond-rewards/#36212b392503

41   https://msbfile03.usc.edu/digitalmeasures/jnunes/intellcont/Endowed%20Progress%20Effect-1.pdf

42   http://fortune.com/2016/09/08/unbanked-americans-fdic/

43   https://icardpromotions.com/visa-incentive-card/

44   https://www.investopedia.com/articles/investing/121715/future-retail-not-big-box-stores.asp

45   Hein, K., and V. Alonzo. "This is what we want." Incentive, 1998, pp. 40-47.

46   http://faculty.chicagobooth.edu/workshops/marketing/pdf/ShafferArkes.pdf

47   https://www.giftcertificates.com/content/documents/GC_Cash_vs_Non-Cash_Awards.pdf

48   https://www.irs.gov/publications/p525

Made in the USA
Monee, IL
19 January 2024

52039755R00159